ROUTLEDGE LIBRARY EDITIONS:
THE VICTORIAN WORLD

Volume 29

A VICTORIAN CHILDHOOD

A VICTORIAN CHILDHOOD

ANNABEL HUTH JACKSON

LONDON AND NEW YORK

First published in 1932 by Methuen & Co. Ltd.

This edition first published in 2016
by Routledge
2 Park Square, Milton Park, Abingdon, Oxon OX14 4RN

and by Routledge
711 Third Avenue, New York, NY 10017

Routledge is an imprint of the Taylor & Francis Group, an informa business

© 1932 Annabel Huth Jackson

All rights reserved. No part of this book may be reprinted or reproduced or utilised in any form or by any electronic, mechanical, or other means, now known or hereafter invented, including photocopying and recording, or in any information storage or retrieval system, without permission in writing from the publishers.

Trademark notice: Product or corporate names may be trademarks or registered trademarks, and are used only for identification and explanation without intent to infringe.

British Library Cataloguing in Publication Data
A catalogue record for this book is available from the British Library

ISBN: 978-1-138-66565-1 (Set)
ISBN: 978-1-315-61965-1 (Set) (ebk)
ISBN: 978-1-138-64169-3 (Volume 29) (hbk)
ISBN: 978-1-315-63030-4 (Volume 29) (ebk)

Publisher's Note
The publisher has gone to great lengths to ensure the quality of this reprint but points out that some imperfections in the original copies may be apparent.

Disclaimer
The publisher has made every effort to trace copyright holders and would welcome correspondence from those they have been unable to trace.

A VICTORIAN CHILDHOOD

BY
ANNABEL HUTH JACKSON
(*née* GRANT DUFF)

WITH 13 ILLUSTRATIONS

METHUEN & CO. LTD.
36 ESSEX STREET W.C.
LONDON

First Published in 1932

PRINTED IN GREAT BRITAIN

LIST OF ILLUSTRATIONS

	FACING PAGE
ANNABEL JACKSON AT TWENTY .	*Frontispiece*
LADY GRANT DUFF WITH HER SON ADRIAN . .	4
ANNABEL JACKSON AT FOUR YEARS OLD . .	8
EDWARD WEBSTER	12
ADRIAN GRANT DUFF	36
LADY GRANT DUFF AND ANNABEL JACKSON BETWEEN THE AGES OF 10–11	72
JAMES GRANT DUFF OF EDEN	80
SIR MOUNTSTUART GRANT DUFF, SIR JOHN HANBURY WILLIAMS, AND CAPTAIN ARTHUR BAGOT	96
GOVERNMENT HOUSE, OOTACAMUND, AND GOVERNMENT HOUSE, MADRAS	102
PET ELEPHANT	120
DOROTHEA BEALE	134
ALISE GRANT DUFF, LATER MADAME OBRIST .	176

v

ANNABEL JACKSON AT TWENTY

"The Ear that heareth the Reproof of Life abideth among the wise."

Proverbs xv. 31.

A VICTORIAN CHILDHOOD

CHAPTER I

ALL people who possess a memory should write their recollections when they reach the age of sixty. Even if their lives have been apparently uninteresting, they are of importance to their grandchildren and great-grandchildren. A dull grandfather is better than no grandfather at all, and this holds good in the present century more than it did at any time before. Formerly tradition was an accepted thing; every boy and girl listened to the stories their forbears told them, and amassed most of what is known of wisdom and history in this way. There was no such thing as a generation which knew nothing of what the generation before it had thought, and felt, and learnt; and the store-house of the world's wisdom was kept supplied. Now a spirit has arisen which we can only call, because of the nation which has most carried it into

A VICTORIAN CHILDHOOD

force, Bolshevist. That spirit dislikes tradition and says that our only chance of happiness is to scrap everything that the world has learnt and begin afresh. Many people believe that this is impossible, but it is terribly true that it can be done. Nothing is so easy as to wipe out the preceding generation. There must have been an immense number of cultures in the past that have left nothing behind them, to the world's permanent loss.

This is my excuse for writing down many things which will interest nobody except my own children. If every one wrote their memoirs most would eventually be burnt, but many details would be preserved for which future generations would be grateful. For I do not believe that the present Bolshevistic point of view raging in England and on the Continent will endure; there is bound to be a reaction, and then all that can be collected to tell of the past will come into its own again.

The first thing I remember distinctly is sitting on the lawn in front of the house we lived in then, Hampden House, the seat of the Earl of Buckinghamshire. I must have been about three and a half and it was

A VICTORIAN CHILDHOOD

hot weather. I was so small that the daisies came up round my fat legs. There was a constant discussion between my parents on the subject of daisies—my mother preferred the lawns shorn like velvet but my father loved the daisies. On this occasion my mother was sitting near me on the grass, and I remember thinking how beautiful she was and how beautiful the sun was. I remember running into the laurels afterwards and biting one of the leaves and I can still recall the queer taste of prussic acid.

At the back of the house were cedars and all that summer I heard the call of the peacocks as they went to bed in the branches. I also remember a dreadful altercation with my nurse. We had an argument, I saying that toads did sit on toadstools, and she that they did not. I surreptitiously caught a toad and put it on a toadstool under the cedars, where it remained, too frightened to move, and then I took her to see it. She smacked me thoroughly, having seen through the ruse. There was a tame toad at Hampden, who lived in the hollow of an old apple-tree, where we used to go and see him, and my brothers gave him slugs every morning. There was a very old gardener with a long beard called Lily. He grew mushrooms under a copy of the Ten Commandments, which had been removed from the village church on some occasion. He produced wonderful mushrooms and years afterwards I heard my mother say that he thought it was something to do with the virtue of the Ten Commandments. There was a fountain and I remember one of my brothers trying to sail on it in a tub and falling in. My mother had it filled up after that with earth and Arthur Hughes did a charming old-fashioned picture of her sitting by the fountain with a peacock and my brother Adrian.

Hampden was very haunted and though the servants were strictly forbidden to speak to the children about such things, we knew that there was something odd about it. One day Adrian took me down the passage and we peeped into the haunted room. Sir Louis Mallet, the father of the present Sir Louis, was badly frightened in that room by a sense of terror and by hearing a woman in a silk dress swish past his bed. He was so scared that he left his dressing-room and spent the night in another room. When I was older I have often heard my mother

LADY GRANT DUFF WITH HER SON ADRIAN

A VICTORIAN CHILDHOOD

relate her experiences there. She was, I think, a medium, for she had a very curious psychic sense. Her boudoir lay right at the end of a long series of sitting-rooms, next a staircase which led to the haunted room. Every night at ten o'clock she would hear a girl's light footsteps run along the passage and down the staircase. If the door was unlocked, it would burst open, if locked some one would fumble with the handle. My father was in London for the session and she was an extraordinarily brave woman. She bore it for three months and then changed her sitting-room.

On another occasion her Blenheim spaniel ran down the passage to the great hall very late one winter night. She called, but as he did not come back, she followed him. To her astonishment the whole place, which was generally lit from a big sconce of candles in the middle of the hall, was brilliantly lighted. Her first thought was, 'The servants have left the lights on and we shall be burned in our beds.'

Then looking up she saw the sconce was unlighted, and the dog came shivering and crouched near her skirt as if it were scared.

She admitted that she had not the courage to go on down the passage to the hall but went back and locked her door.

As a girl she was a friend of the branch of the Hobart Hampden family who did not then hold the title. She often stayed with Lady Hobart and Mrs. Bacon, then Miss Carrs. George Cameron Hampden, the heir to the title, lived abroad, and was a distant cousin, so my mother's friends had no thought of inheriting. One night when staying with them she had a very strange dream. She dreamt that she married and went to live at Hampden House, which she did not know then, but had often heard talked about. Whilst she was there a son was born to her, and shortly after, the property returned to her branch of the Hobart Hampdens, through a box which stood in the front hall. She went down to breakfast full of her dream and they all chaffed her very much. 'But what was the box like?' asked Lady Hobart. 'Were there papers in it?'—'I do not know,' said my mother, 'I know it was very heavy, it had to be put on trestles.' . . . 'But what was the shape?'—'I cannot remember,' said my mother, 'I only know that the property came

A VICTORIAN CHILDHOOD

back to your branch through a box which stood in the front hall.'

Years after she married, Hampden House came into the market and my father took it for five years. Whilst he was there a brother was born. Cameron Hampden died abroad, his body was brought back and laid in the front hall on trestles and the other branch of the family came in for the title. I have heard both Lady Hobart and my mother tell this story and they agreed in every particular. It seems to me that I vaguely remember the hall at Hampden, hung with black, and being very frightened. But I expect that this was told me later.

I cannot have been more than four and a half when my nurse Mrs. Cave, of whom I was very fond, fell ill and went to the seaside, and I was left in the charge of Nurse Maunder, who was a Baptist and a typical Calvinist, cruel, rigid, but with the virtues of her defects, clean, absolutely honest, hard working, and conscientious. I had been very grubby and was taken to my mother for punishment, and she thrashed me with a small rhinoceros-hide whip with a gold top, which she used when riding. I do not suppose she hurt me very much, though I thought she did. But far worse were the agonies of shame I suffered, both at the time and for weeks afterwards. I scarcely dared walk round the garden because I felt all the gardeners knew, and when Mrs. Cave came back and I told her about the episode, I sobbed and sobbed till she cried too. Shortly after, she went away and I heard later that she was supposed not to be quite normal. But I adored her and I was broken-hearted. Nurse Maunder reigned in her stead.

At three and a half I was put on a pony, Peri, a Shetland, and went for delightful rides with a groom called Harry, and a dog called Spot. I still have a little old photograph of myself at this period in the long dangerous riding-habit that was considered essential. When Peri and Pixie first came to Eden, my father's house in Scotland, from the Shetland Isles, they would not touch hay, and seaweed had to be procured for them. They gradually learnt to eat hay.

I remember on my fourth birthday being made to read to my grandfather, Edward Webster, out of a book called *My Mother* which contained a story called 'The Dog's Dinner Party' and one called 'The Peacock's

ANNABEL JACKSON AT FOUR YEARS OLD

At Home' and the aforesaid 'My Mother', a poem no one remembers now except for the delightful parody about Gladstone and Huxley in which occurs the much-quoted verse:

> 'Who filled his soul with carnal pride?
> Who made him say that Moses lied
> About the little hare's inside?
> The Devil.'

It must have been a few months after this that I was taken down to Ealing to see my grandfather Webster when he was dying and I remember being lifted up to kiss him. He was beautiful even as an old man. He and his brother were so handsome that old men in Derbyshire used to say that when the Websters walked into church people would stand up to look at them. He lived in a little house called North Lodge, on Ealing Green, with my grandmother who was a Miss Ainsworth, of Smithills Hall, Bolton-le-Moors, a house that later played such a big part in my life.

A few months after his death Adrian and I and the baby Hampden were sent to Ealing whilst my mother went to Rome. We liked being there, but I remember my winter was poisoned by a dreadful horror of bears. I used to dream about bears and I was always thinking that there were bears either under or sitting on my bed. The part that dreams play in the life of an imaginative child is now known to be very important. But then, whenever one spoke of dreams one was told not to be a silly girl and never to bore people by recounting one's visions. I always made my own children tell me all their dreams and they were enormously helpful in teaching me about their characters and how to train them. I know many mothers who did the same thing through sheer intuition long before Freud and Jung told the world how vital these observations were. The study is an old one; these men are only working on the same lines as Joseph and Daniel in the Old Testament.

It was during that winter that I began to dream consistently and usually very frightening dreams. As I said, many were about bears, but one which was to me more alarming than any centred on the word 'magic', which I had picked up somewhere. It would be a little coil of rope that would terrify me sometimes, or some other quite unimportant thing, but always somebody would say, 'Ah, yes, that is magic' —and I would be scared. I cannot remember whether it was that year or the next that I began to have a dream which left me quite exhausted in the morning. I thought that I was sitting in a boat being rowed down a river. The man who was rowing me had a cowl over his face like a monk and I could only see his eyes, which were intensely bright. He never said a word, but he rowed and rowed, and as he rowed the river got narrower and narrower until at last it came between two cliffs and it wound on and became like a ditch and the cliffs came together, and I woke screaming, or sometimes to find myself head downwards in the bed with the clothes right over me. The last time I had this dream I must have been about seven years old and when we reached the narrow part the man stood up and said, 'Now you will see me no more until you see faces upon the trees.' Imagine my terror when, a week later, my brother Adrian said, 'Isn't that like a face on the chestnut-tree?' But I have never had that dream again.

It was when I was eight or nine that I began to have lovely dreams. I suppose

A VICTORIAN CHILDHOOD

I got stronger and less nervous by that time and more able to cope with outside things. A small child is so helpless and overwhelmed. Perhaps the greatest moment in its life is when the child suddenly realizes that it can stand up against the objects animate and inanimate which till then have been too much for it.

At Ealing I remember picking flowered grasses and Herb Robert, and the excitement of finding something green at last after the long winter. There was a monkey-puzzle tree in the garden and we admired this immensely, though it was like all monkey-puzzles, a hideous thing. Few people had them then and we thought it a great asset.

My grandmother had a couple of fields and an old horse which used to take her about in a brougham. She had an old butler called Peprel, an old maid called Vine and an old cook. It was very peaceful there and whenever I went I wished that I was an only child. I was sometimes allowed to play very quietly in the drawing-room where my grandmother sat by the fire in an arm-chair, wearing a frilled tulle cap and black dress with a white collar and

EDWARD WEBSTER

cuffs of tulle. I never took any toys to the drawing-room, but my grandmother let me play with a little silver stork seal and a small bronze figure of the Venus of Milo and a bronze inkstand made to represent the temple of Vesta. My grandmother had an old friend called Mrs. Minty who lived next door, and two old Miss Percivals came in from their house opposite. I believe they were the sisters of the Spencer Percival who was assassinated. The ground and all around it is now covered with horrid little villas, but then it was almost country and very charming.

I read *Evenings at Home* in that drawing-room and Bewick's *Birds* and Miss Mitford's *Our Village* and the *History of the Robins*.

My mother's father's family were a wild lot. I think it was her great-great-grandfather who played away first his money, then his wife's jewellery, and finally his estate in a single night, and walked out of his home next morning penniless.

One of her forebears was a niece of Dr. Taylor, the friend of Dr. Johnson. She was very foolish and ran away with a handsome gypsy, and her family quite naturally never saw her again. She went to another county and lived in great poverty, and of course had a large family. But old Dr. Taylor, hearing that one of her sons was a decent human being, sent for the lad and made him a footman in his establishment. When Dr. Taylor's will was to be read and all the relations were assembled for the purpose, William came into the room carrying coals to make up the fire. 'Go upstairs and take off your livery, William,' said the old family lawyer, 'for you will never wear it again.' Dr. Taylor had left him everything. He went up to Oxford, where he made charming friends and did very well. He eventually married and became my great-grandfather.

From Ealing we went to 4 Queen's Gate Gardens, which at that time belonged to my father. It was so country then that he used to say to the cabman when he came out of the House of Commons at night, 'Drive along the Cromwell Road till you come to a hedge and then turn right.'

It was this spring that Adrian and I had measles in London and were nursed by an Irish nurse who danced jigs and was extraordinarily amusing. We admired her in-

A VICTORIAN CHILDHOOD

tensely and when she was sent away for being very drunk we were sorry.

After the illness most of our toys were burnt and we were annoyed because china ones as well as stuffed ones went. Adrian had a straw tiger and I a china cock. Both of us agreed that the tiger ought to go and was legitimate prey for the authorities, but that the destruction of the cock was wanton cruelty. I can see him sitting up in a flannel nightgown singing a dirge for all the sacrificed toys.

CHAPTER II

ABOUT this time a charming woman came to us as a governess for six months, called Mrs. French. She was a very pretty and attractive creature, and quite young. She had married at sixteen, and, when she first arrived, cannot have been more than twenty-two or three. Her small boy, Louis French, who was about our age, stayed for that Easter at Knebworth, which my father had rented from Lord Lytton. She was kind and good, and I remember her with affectionate gratitude.

That was my first conscious spring, and I can still feel the thrill of waking up in the early morning to hear the starlings outside my window. I shall never forget the clear coo-ee of the starlings, I like it better than the song of any bird.

It was at Knebworth that I found my first primrose, and later in the year the great trusses of lilac and laburnum and heavy scented peonies were a real joy to me. It was a perfect garden for children. There was a Chinese garden, a Greek garden with the Three Graces in the middle, a Rosery and everything that the eighteenth century could imagine of beauty. In the house there were circular rooms set in the towers and a gilt Calvary which filled us with terror and emotion. There were flowers and fruit made in stone, and curious old portraits and a banqueting hall with men in armour standing round. There was also a terrible bookcase full of occult books which we children were not allowed to take out. But once one of my brothers showed me some of the pictures, and I can remember a fearful face with a red beard. Lord Arthur Russell told me, many years later, that when a small boy he was taken to Knebworth by his mother. Lady William told him that whatever he saw during the visit that surprised him, he was not to ask questions, but to wait till he got home. Next morning he was in the big hall sitting by his mother having breakfast with many other guests when a strange-looking old gentleman in a shabby dressing-gown came in and walked slowly round the table, staring at each of the guests in turn. He heard his mother's neighbour whisper to her, 'Do not take any notice, he thinks he is invisible.' It was Lord Lytton himself. He certainly put his acquired knowledge to good account, for he wrote one of the most terrifying ghost stories in English.

There was a haunted room at Knebworth and a woman used to be heard spinning. I once slept there with my mother. I cannot remember why, but I think it was because one of the children was suspected of having some infectious complaint, anyway I did sleep there and woke up terrified just as my mother was coming up to bed about eleven. She found me screaming with fright and I remember her taking me out of the bed and putting me in her bath to soothe me. I never knew why I was frightened, but years afterwards, Madame de Navarro, formerly Miss Mary Anderson, told me a curious story of something that happened when she occupied that room. Her maid was sleeping next door. She had not been very long in bed before she heard what appeared to be a man in chains crawling over the floor and sighing violently. The chains clanked as he moved and his sighs were quite terrible. She called out to the maid, 'Oh, Alice, do you hear it?' and the maid answered, 'Oh, Miss Mary, for God's sake come to me, I cannot move.' Miss Anderson slipped out of bed just as whatever it was got to the bed. She reached the maid's room and they both escaped into the corridor by another door. Everything was in total darkness and they did not know what to do, but the maid remembered having seen the governess' room whilst on a tour of inspection the preceding afternoon. The governess was very kind and gave them blankets and they slept on her floor. In the morning Lady Lytton begged them not to say anything about it because Mrs. Villiers, her mother, who was staying in the house, had had exactly the same experience the year before and would be very frightened.

I give the story exactly as Madame de Navarro told it to me. I was never frightened at Knebworth myself except in that one room, and on one other occasion, the first few days we were there, I remember being frightened. I do not know why, but this happened on the other side of the passage.

The house was surrounded by a great park full of fallow deer. Once the hunt came through the park and killed one of the deer and I remember the place where the deer was killed seemed to us like a horrible murder spot. We never went near it without shuddering.

There was a chain of little lakes in the park and a charming cottage on one of them, where the old Lord Lytton used to write his novels, and there were great bulrushes and kingfishers.

The house was watched over by an old housekeeper called Mrs. Tate and there were eighteen gardeners who kept the place in order, many of whom were friends and some enemies. The head gardener was called Kipling and we admired him very much. I remember a dreadful episode when one of my brothers told me to tell the ugliest gardener that he was an Adonis. I did not in the least know what it meant and fulfilled my task, only to be severely punished by my nurse for having been impertinent, besides making old Dennis an enemy for life.

I did not like brothers. I do not remember it, but one of the early dramas of my life was when I ran for my second brother with a carving knife, caught up from the table. The butler seized me from behind and held my two arms until I dropped it. No doubt my brother richly deserved what

A VICTORIAN CHILDHOOD

I intended for him. They were always teasing me and preventing me from living my own separate, quite happy existence. I fancy they were early victims of the dreadful 'public-school spirit' idea which has made the English from one of the most self-reliant nations in the world to one of the most helpless. Teamwork, *esprit de corps*, and all the other shibboleths invented to create the herd mentality, were rubbed into the poor things at their various educational establishments and in their holidays they tried to pass them on to me. But I was a confirmed Individualist, and small and weak as I was, I fought as long as I could. It was a joke in the family that when I was too small to know better and I began to say my prayers at night I used to murmur 'God bless brothers (not Evie)'. But I always later prayed for them all in orthodox fashion.

They invented a game called Doggyland and this comprised a code of laws, a geography and a history which one was expected to assimilate, and also an immense amount of fighting. My eldest brother, who was a good deal weaker and gentler than the other two, was always put as my partner against the other ones. We fought with long lances, with short daggers and with swords, all cut of different lengths of wood and pointed. I was always terrified and loathed it all with a bitter hatred, especially when I was a prisoner and liable to be hurt. Why we did not put each other's eyes out I have never understood. My favourite game of Little Houses, which consisted of quietly keeping house and pretending to go out and hunt for food, was considered a crime, and I was punished whenever I played it. The holidays were a nightmare. But fortunately the other boys were away for a great part of the year and when Adrian and I were alone we were good friends, but it took me years to get over my terror of Evelyn. I do not believe for one moment that he realized what he was doing. But he was taught the accursed system of ill-treating the weak at school and considered me fair game. He was by far the ablest of my brothers and it was a tragedy that he should have been warped in early life. He grew up to be a very clever and amusing person, and he married a most delightful girl, Edith Bonham, with whom he was supremely happy.

I asked two Eton men of different ages the other day, if they had ever, in their

A VICTORIAN CHILDHOOD

whole school experience, known of a case of a boy or boys standing up for one that the herd were persecuting. They hesitated for a moment and then said, 'I am afraid not, it is not in boy nature.' I believe that is totally untrue, or rather that a better point of view could easily be inculcated in boys if their elders were less hypocritical and less unobservant. The average house master has not the remotest idea of what his boys are really like, and when he has he is too scared of unpleasantness to take the bull by the horns. He prates about schoolboy honour whereas schoolboy honour is merely the astute device whereby the bully and the law breaker can insure immunity. The average man would have been a better creature had he never been to school. I do not know what wiser system could be evolved, but I think what is needed is a more intelligent type of master, especially of house master. Many mothers know a good deal about the conditions in school, but they are so afraid of getting their own pet lamb into trouble that they say nothing. And the conspiracy of silence goes on and the most splendid raw material in the world is in many cases ruined.

A VICTORIAN CHILDHOOD

During one holiday when I was about six and a half, I heard my nurse discussing a case of suicide which had occurred. A man had thrown himself out of a window. It was the summer holidays and I was being persecuted. Being also a very vain child, it struck me that I could get away from my brothers, and at the same time do something very grand by emulating the gentleman who had just very literally paved the way. So I climbed on to the roof and when caught by an indignant nursery-maid who asked me in great horror what I thought I was doing, I replied simply and firmly, 'I am going to commit suicide.' She seized me by the leg and I was ignominiously dragged down. The case was considered so grave that I was taken to my mother, who scolded me very much and tried to explain what a very wicked thing it was to do. My father was fortunately there or things might have been worse. I was tied up to a table when indoors for a week and led for walks on a long string. But the episode helped a good deal, for it made me realize that there was a way out, and I was too young to comprehend what superhuman courage is required to take one's own life and also too young to know that whatever one scamps here has got to be gone through somewhere else.

It was at Knebworth that I first became aware of people outside the actual nursery potentates. Of these the one I remember most clearly was Sir John Lubbock, afterwards Lord Avebury. He was a very constant visitor and we adored him. He was even more remarkable for his great character and goodness than for his great intelligence. He never came to see us without bringing Adrian and me a present of some kind, and I remember one dismal day when I, knowing that he had something for me, went into his bedroom to hunt for it, a mean trick. I saw on his table a large bottle of Eau de Cologne. I had heard people say that it was delicious, so I took enormous gulps and lay on the floor writhing in agony for some time. I did not dare tell any one about it, so went about with a little blistered mouth for days, feeling very ill. It firmly convinced me that as my Calvinist nurse used to tell me, 'There were all-seeing eyes to punish sin.'

We were very fond of the local clergyman and his children, the Jennings', who often came to tea. The little church at

A VICTORIAN CHILDHOOD

Knebworth stood in the park and still had the square pews which are now abolished. During the interminable Matins to which Adrian and I were taken, we amused ourselves by choosing who would kneel bolt upright, as was the fashion with devout people in those days, and who would fling themselves on the cushions and go to sleep. We became extraordinarily clever at knowing by the look of the guests, which would do which. I think more Anglican children are choked off religion by being taken to Choral Matins than by any other means. If they were all taken to Mass at once they would not dislike Church the way they do. Mothers tell me that they cannot possibly understand and that it is therefore a mistake to take them to it. But they are aware that something great is going on and as Mass only lasts for half an hour they can keep their attention fixed for that time. And if they are told that this is the service that is to be the constant re-acting of the drama of our Lord's Redemption of the World, they very soon realize the importance of it. 'The proof of the pudding is in the eating', to put it vulgarly, and one never finds a case of Roman Catholic children who do not go to church willingly and I have never seen children brought up on really Catholic lines who minded going to Mass. Still I would far rather children went to Choral Matins than that they did not go at all, or merely went to Sunday School. The habit of churchgoing should be inculcated very early if it is to resist the immense pull the other way directly the child is old enough to take a share in grown-up amusements.

About this time Mrs. French, whom we liked so much, was superseded by a German, Fräulein Reinking, who was the worst example of her class, a bigoted Roman Catholic, an ill-tempered woman whose nerves had been shattered by successive generations of children, and a very uninteresting teacher with no merits except that of being a strict disciplinarian. I have seen her break a ruler over Adrian's back, but her punishment for me was to shut me up in a dark cupboard. I was not in the least afraid of the dark, but I was terrified of beetles and always thought there were beetles in it. She also constantly sent us to bed as a punishment directly after tea, I think as a means of getting us out of the way for the evening, and it was very trying on long beautiful summer evenings to have to go to bed at five, besides meaning that I suffered from insomnia in later life from having an irregular bedtime. We got very knowing about concealing books under our mattresses. My whole early life was a perpetual fight against authority.

I was very often scolded when I was little for inventing stories, especially for saying I had seen things that I had not seen. It is very difficult to know how far a child's imagination magnifies and diminishes the object, and I remember very distinctly thinking I had seen a quite enormous puff-ball as big as a basin, in the park. I told Fräulein Reinking about it and she said she would like to see it. I took her out, firmly believing that the puff-ball was there, and when we got to the place there was quite an ordinary puff-ball, as I had to admit myself. I was severely punished and had to go about for days with 'Liar' printed on my back, which was a terrible punishment to me, and what enraged me most was that I was certain the puff-ball had been there, and that Providence had removed it and put a smaller one in its place just to get me into trouble.

I remember on another occasion seeing

a little round house with a thatched roof. When I went round it I could not find a way in. I was very excited and went and told Adrian about it. He also saw the little house and we were just going to try to get in when the nursery-maid called us and we had to leave it and go in for tea. The next day we started out for the house and there was no house there, and we never found it again. Did I imagine it and pass my imagination on to Adrian so that he saw it too? I have never been able to make up my mind, but children are often punished for saying they have seen things which really came from their imaginations. There is the historic story of Miss Bates for instance, which I tell here, though to many it will be a chestnut.

Miss Bates was a little girl of six who romanced about what she had seen. Her mother told her that the next time she told a lie she would have to go to bed after tea. A few days afterwards Miss Bates came in from her usual walk and said, 'Oh, Mummum, I have seen a most 'normous lion in the park.' Her mother said, 'Lucy darling, I am afraid you did not see a lion in the park.'—'Oh, yes I did.' So Lucy's mother said sadly that she must go to bed directly after tea and when dismissing her she added, 'I hope, darling, that when you say your prayers you will ask God's pardon for telling that dreadful story.' When she went up to kiss her good night she asked, 'Did you remember, Lucy, to ask God's forgiveness for having told a lie?'—'Yes, Mummum, I did, and He said, "Don't mention it, Miss Bates, I have often seen that yellow dog Myself and it is very like a lion."'

I think I was naturally difficult, but Adrian was a good child and truthful, and he was simply made naughty by the treatment he received. We had a very happy life when we were alone together, but I never remember a comfortable moment in the schoolroom or the nursery and our meals were detestable.

We endured one particularly flagrant instance of injustice one day when Nurse Maunder had said we were not to go to the kitchen garden and steal fruit, which we often did. But, meeting Kipling the head gardener, he gave us each apples and we devoured them and were caught red-handed. Marched off to the nursery we were whipped

A VICTORIAN CHILDHOOD

and put to bed. In vain we shrieked that Kipling had given us the apples. It was all of no avail. Adrian very sensibly flung himself on the ground and yelled, but I was in such a rage that I refused to yell and of course got a far worse hiding for 'being stubborn'. The shame of the punishment was bad enough, but the fearful sense of injustice was worse. Kipling was grown up, they were Kipling's apples, he had given them to us, therefore we should by all laws human and divine, have been allowed to eat them. Adrian explained to me next day that it was idiotic not to yell when you were chastised and that all grown-ups hit one harder if one did not.

I am sure Nurse Maunder thought she was doing her duty. And after bringing up four children and agonizingly trying to see their point of view and to give them a beautiful time and a happy life, I must now admit that the previous generation to mine seems to have accomplished more with my contemporaries than we have done with our children. Their methods may have been faulty, but the result was better. I suppose all human beings think that they might have been splendid people had their education and environment been different. But as one grows older one realizes that probably most fathers and mothers tried just as hard as one has done oneself, and possibly failed as dismally.

My mother was always an overworked woman, having too many children and being also busy with my father's public life. Until I was eight and a half I often had a hard time. That spring my mother took me to Algiers with her. The rest of the party consisted of my father, Sir John Lubbock, and his daughter, afterwards Mrs. Buxton. I told my mother a little about our nursery conditions then and she sent away Miss Reinking and Nurse Maunder on our return, and kind Mrs. Carpenter came in their stead.

This visit to Algiers was one of the most delightful and important events in my life. Our villa at Mustapha Supérieure was an exquisite old Moorish house with a great courtyard and the garden was too beautiful to be true, with hedges of rosemary and lavender on which a child could lie full length without breaking them down. We had a French cook, and an old couple who lived there and were caretakers, did the work.

A VICTORIAN CHILDHOOD

It was my first experience of the East and of sunlight and I think I was drunk with joy whilst the three weeks lasted. The gardener had a little daughter, and she and I chattered French and stuffed ourselves with loquats and dates and played about in the garden. The sea was always blue and I can still remember the little irises coming up in the sand.

On the way back I was terribly seasick in the Gulf of Lyons and my mother laughed because in the middle of one of my worst spasms I came across a word I did not know in the book I was trying to read, *Peter Parley*, and asked her, 'Mother, what does oscillation mean?'

We stopped in Paris and went to see Mrs. Augustus Craven, who played such a rôle in my father's life and whom from that day became a factor in mine. We also went to see a cousin of my mother's who was a nun in Notre Dame de Sion and I remember assisting at the Catholic Service of Benediction, and seeing the girls in their blue dresses filing in with white veils on their heads, and how I was impressed by the intensity of worship which I apprehended for the first time. Cousin Anna Jackson afterwards ran away from this convent in a very dramatic way.

Madame Craven was the daughter of the Comte de la Ferronays, a diplomat at the Court of Naples before the court was abolished. She married an English diplomat, Augustus Craven, and as they were very badly off she took up writing early in life. Her novels are very well known in pious circles in France and were at one time a good deal read in England. They are old-fashioned now, but they have great charm and distinction. Her most important book, *Le Récit d'une Soeur*, translated in England as *A Sister's Story*, was the chronicle of the lives of her own people, especially of Alexandrine de la Ferronays, the wife of her brother Albert. The whole family and their connexions represented all that was best in the old French régime, gifted, amusing, pious, and witty. They formed an almost ideal society to which it was very difficult for strangers or foreigners to gain admission, but my father and his friend Mrs. Bishop, who afterwards wrote a life of Mrs. Craven, were allowed into the charmed circle and Mrs. Augustus Craven became one of his greatest friends. One of her best-known relations was her sister's son, Albert de Mun, the Christian Socialist, much appreciated in English political life in the 'seventies and 'eighties, and the Duc de Blacas, whom I met later, was the most charming and complete type of the French aristocrat whom I have ever seen.

When I got home, as I said before, Nurse Maunder's régime was changed and Mrs. Carpenter, who was as stupid as a cow but very kind and let us do anything we liked, took her place. We had an old tutor called Herr Hoering who came in to give us music lessons. He was supposed to give us German lessons too, but as he had forgotten his German and not learnt English I do not think we learnt very much. I also had French lessons and the French mistress, an expert, introduced us to the *Bibliothèque Rose*. How I loved the *Petites Filles Modèles* and the *Malheurs de Sophie* and all the other enchanting works of Madame de Ségur.

Adrian was now at Mr. West's school at Bournemouth where the elder boys had been. We had been constant companions and very great friends up to this time whenever the two elder boys were away and he had not to show his manhood by ill-treating girls, and I was horrified and miserable when he came back for the first holidays and I realized that he had *really* learnt to despise girls and no longer wanted to play with me. I went through several days of anguish and then put him out of my mind. We never were the least intimate after that, though I always had a great respect for him.

He was a fine fellow, and a first-rate soldier. 'He was killed at the Battle of the Aisne on the 14th September 1914. Some time after the Regiment had been deployed and engaged, it became imperative that a certain locality should be held against the German counter-attack. Having none of his battalion now left in reserve, Lieut.-Colonel Grant Duff, collecting all available men, personally led them forward, and held this important position, but shortly afterwards was wounded mortally.'

All his life it had been his dream to lead the Black Watch into action in some great war, and though his death was an unmixed tragedy for his family and friends, I have always thought he was the most fortunate of us all. Surely to die fairly young in the moment of fulfilment is the supreme luck of life?

ADRIAN GRANT DUFF

A VICTORIAN CHILDHOOD

He was the chief person responsible for the *War Book* which played such a part at the beginning of the Great War. Lord Haldane, whose work for the army has never been sufficiently appreciated, told me once that he thought that my brother had done more than anybody else towards making the English mobilization a success. I copy from my sister-in-law's little Memoir, in *The Bond of Sacrifice*, notes of his activities in this department.

Before 1912 there was practically no co-ordination between the various government departments of this country for the eventuality of war. Even the Admiralty and the War Office made their plans separately. But one or two far-reaching minds had seen the danger of this state of things in our modern world and had begun to attempt some sort of co-operation. In January 1911 a sub-committee on co-ordination was appointed under the Imperial Defence Committee, and when in August of the same year the risk of war with Germany over the Agadir incident revealed our complete unpreparedness the Government realized its enormous importance.

Sir Charles Ottley, the secretary of the Committee of Imperial Defence, was secretary of this Committee, and Colonel Grant Duff, who had been among the foremost in pressing for this inquiry, was the assistant secretary. It was on him that the bulk of the work fell. It was he who, with infinite patience, designed the framework of the *War Book* into which were fitted the full instructions for each Government Office for the action to be taken by them on the outbreak of War concerning every foreseen contingency, such as: 'Mobilization of Naval centres and Signal stations, Protection of vulnerable points, Harbour traffic, certain preliminary stages of Navy and Army mobilization, censorship, control of aliens, treatment of enemy merchantmen in port, Trading with the enemy, Government War Insurance of Shipping and Cargoes, Control of Railways, and many other similar measures, down to such internal arrangements as the suspension of certain acts if found necessary.'

The first edition of the *War Book* was completed by Colonel Grant Duff in May 1912, from the material supplied to him by nine Government Departments. Colonel Grant Duff also edited the second edition dated 18 June 1813 in which eleven Departments were represented and which extended the system to all parts of the British Empire. The *War Book* was finally brought up to date just before the War by his successor, Colonel Longridge. Credit for the *War Book* has been given by Mr. Lloyd George to Sir Maurice Hankey, who after succeeding Sir Charles Ottley in 1918 as Secretary of the C.I.D. was responsible for all the work of the secretariat, but as mentioned in the official *History of the War* (Naval Operations; Corbett), Chapter I, it was Colonel Grant Duff who was responsible for its design. It was he who saw that the various parts really fitted into each other and did most of the work which saved this country from chaos in August 1914 by the extraordinary smoothness and success with which all his arrangements worked out.

Note.—It was for the *War Book* that he was given his C.B. 1913.

A VICTORIAN CHILDHOOD

It takes one a long way from that sunny trip of my childhood to Algiers, of which I have just spoken.

Soon after the Algiers episode Fräulein Schübnall came as governess. We did not like her, but she was a first-rate teacher and she not only taught me German but imbued me with a love of Germany and everything German. She was bad-tempered, and what children particularly dislike, very common, but she had extraordinarily good qualities and one was that she kept us amused and taught us delightful things to do with our hands. She gave me lessons in needlework and knitting and I remember the first Christmas she was with us a splendid ball of wool was wound round small presents so that the more you knitted the sooner you reached the object concealed. This was a great incentive to industry. I only got one sock finished for my father, and presented it to him with pride for Christmas. He told me it was very very beautiful, but I afterwards heard him say to my mother, 'The poor dear child must think I have elephantiasis!'

We also had a very nice English governess called Miss Meymott, afterwards Mrs. Rylands, who has remained a friend till now. It was during her reign that I first cared for music. A choir-boy in our small church next door had shown great promise and had been asked to play the organ. He was quite unusually gifted, besides being a rather handsome and attractive human being. I was about eight at the time he first began to play, and fell violently in love with his personal appearance and still more with his exquisite playing. I became quite devout and went to church every time I possibly could, and I remember when I used to see him in the street, which was bound to happen in a small village such as Twickenham was then, I shivered all over with delicious excitement. I only met him once and that was many years afterwards. I wondered whether I should tell him of my childish adoration. He is now Sir Walter Alcock, organist of Salisbury Cathedral, and has fulfilled the promise he showed as a boy.

It was this autumn that for some reason that I cannot remember, I was left alone at York House with the servants. The younger children, I think, had had some infantile disease and were taken away to the sea by Mrs. Carpenter. Miss Meymott came in every morning, but she was away after four and I was quite alone. I realized for the first time the joy of solitude and I was completely happy. I was able to have my tea as I preferred it, frightfully strong, and having come across Abbé Huc's *Travels in Tibet*, tried drinking it with butter, which he relates as amongst his experiences in that country. I liked it very much; a horrible taste! The nurserymaid, Emma, who was supposed to look after me, left me completely to myself and I knew that as long as I did not break anything, nobody would ask any questions, and I had a beautiful time exploring the house and examining everything with minute attention. Such times are enormously fruitful in a child's life. We hear so much pity for the only child, but we never hear any pity for the child brought up in a herd who prefers to be alone.

CHAPTER III

MY father had a secretary called Miss Bellairs who had a wonderful contralto voice. She also stimulated my love of music and I was always asking her to sing to me. She used to sing 'The Lost Chord' and 'I've been Roaming' and a song of Arthur Sullivan's called 'Guinevere' which delighted me very much. It is curious what chance things impress characters on a child's mind. Lancelot and Guinevere became live characters to me because of that very sentimental and quite unimportant song. Afterwards when I read the *Morte d'Arthur* I felt I was getting back to friends. I suppose, except the Bible, it is the book of all others that most takes hold of a child's mind. I remember reading it for the second time when I was about twenty-three, at a moment when I was living very intensely in many ways myself, and the characters became so much more real to me that I forgot all about my own love affairs and sorrows and felt that King Arthur's knights were more important. Oscar Wilde says somewhere that 'the study of Balzac reduces one's friends to shadows and one's acquaintances to the shadows of shades' and this is also true of the *Morte d'Arthur*. I know no other authors who have this particular quality, though I have heard some people say that they feel the same about Proust.

By the time I was ten I could play the piano a little and was very fond of it, and I could sing quantities of Volkslieder, and I could always pick out anything I wanted to play and make some kind of accompaniment, and I spent much time singing. I also sang all the poems I liked to strange tunes of my own composing, or tunes I had heard. I must have been a very tiresome child.

My father always told the reigning governess to encourage us to read, and I still have a little book given me on my tenth birthday in which to put down everything I had read. When I think of the rubbish that children swallow nowadays, I am thankful that I had parents who simply would not let me read most of the books that were published as suitable for children, for the average, though better than it is now, was often poor. We read Mrs. Ewing, Grimm, Hans Andersen, Christina Rossetti, *Alice in Wonderland* and *Alice Through the Looking-Glass*, George MacDonald, Mrs. Molesworth, Jean Ingelow and Ruskin's *King of the Golden River*, also Baldwin's *Pantheon* which I knew almost by heart. But of all these I cared most for Hans Andersen and George MacDonald's *Fairy Tales*, and I think, to be quite honest, I still like them better than any other books. I learnt an immense lot of poetry and read all through Scott's Poems and I remember reading 'Lucile', by Lord Lytton, and the 'Lady of La Garaye', by Mrs. Norton. My father's theory was that provided a thing was not coarse a child might read it, and I think he was right. The only thing he ever told me not to read was *Don Juan* when I was about twelve, and I had already read it and could not imagine why it was said to be improper. I never dared tell him that I had read it until I was grown up and then he laughed very much.

Prompted on the one hand by Nurse Maunder the Baptist, and on the other by

Miss Reinking the Roman, I became very religious about seven years old. That birthday my father gave me the *Imitation of Christ* and Adrian and I read it every day with Miss Reinking, being allowed to choose the passages we preferred. I regret to say that we always chose the shortest passages. But some of the marvellous prose and the white-hot passion of the writer entered into my consciousness and it has always remained one of the books I care for most. Also, from it Christ became a living figure, though I always imagined Him as a Knight in armour, ready to help at any moment, and able quite literally to move a lion from one's path. I hated God, who seemed to me cruel and waiting round every corner to punish me. I remember walking round the nursery table one day in a rage, saying, 'I hate God, I hate God and I hope I *will* go to Hell'—to the horror of Nurse Maunder who gave me a large dose of castor oil, a favourite punishment.

One unfortunate day I said something to my mother about Christ being able to take lions out of one's way and she, quite unthinkingly, said, 'Oh, but you must not think of Christ as anything supernatural.'

Meaning, I suppose, that I must not believe in miracles. I was dumbfounded, and I felt it must be true because my mother had said so, and I went about utterly miserable and with my faith in ruins. Nothing could, I am sure, have been further from my mother's thoughts than to disturb my faith, but it only shows how careful one must be with young children. Arthur also laughed at me about the same time for thinking that thunder was the voice of God, and that gave me another shake. Gradually I became a frank little Pagan and went back to Baldwin's *Pantheon* as a more certain guide. I liked Apollo better than Christ and on a tree-stump in the garden I erected an altar, and here I kept a gallipot full of fresh water which I changed every day, and bunches of flowers. I used occasionally to steal bread and wine left in the glasses after lunch, and offer it up to my divinity. I really believed in Apollo and in beauty being the only thing that mattered. Every kind of beauty appealed to me and I hated ugliness with a hatred which has grown more intense with every year of my life. There is no excuse for it, God made the world beautiful and it is only the senseless idiocy of human beings that has reduced it to what it is now, a scrapheap. Most people prefer ugliness. It is so much easier to be ugly, and in admiring ugliness you not only drag down what in your inmost soul you know is superior to you, but you at once gain a reputation for intelligence and discrimination with the mob, who asks nothing better than to admire its ugly self.

All that summer we were allowed to run about with bare feet, I forget why, but it was a great pleasure and our health benefited in a most amazing way.

It was about this year that we went down to the sea to stay with my grandmother who had taken a house at Seaford. I had seen the sea at Algiers, but I had never played in it or paddled in it, and we were extraordinarily happy. My grandmother's butler Peprel used to take us out to collect winkles and we afterwards had scrumptious teas in the housekeeper's room, to our great delight.

One of the things modern children miss is the intimacy with loyal old servants. The old-fashioned type who were very close to the children, but who never thought of taking a liberty with them, has absolutely gone and it is now a choice between never seeing them at all or putting up with that dreadful familiarity which must be bad for both parties.

One night I woke up with the moonlight flooding my room and I crept out of bed to the window and saw for the first time the moonlight on the sea. I can still recollect the amazement and wonder and joy which it gave me and the vision remained for several days. I never woke again during my stay and it was many months before I saw moonlight on the sea again.

During this visit I had my first beautiful dream. It was of a most exquisite country by the sea, lying in the moonlight, but brighter than any moon that ever shone on land or ocean. And my companion there was a creature like a Greek god, Prince Archer he was called. I suppose that it was inspired by Baldwin's *Pantheon*. I realized then, once for all, that dreams are more perfect than any waking experience. I used to look forward to the night as much more important than the day. I have never lost the conviction that it is so, and though, alas, it is very easy to lose the habit of 'dreaming true' as George du Maurier puts

A VICTORIAN CHILDHOOD

it, all the early part of my life I not only learnt enormously from dreams, but also had great happiness in them, happiness that no waking experiences have ever equalled.

Mrs. French had taught me poetry from five onwards. We had learnt from a book called *Beauties of the English Poets* and I could say Roger's 'If ever you should come to Modena', and 'The Cave of Despair' from Spencer's *Faerie Queen*. A curious selection. I also learnt quantities of Longfellow who was then my favourite poet as he should be with every child. No other poet has just the qualities a child needs, great moral feeling, an eye for the picturesque and dramatic, a historic sense and a deep love of nature and humanity. This combined with very easy versification, which does not tire or weary a child's memory. I can hear my own children saying, 'Oh, no one considers Longfellow a poet now.' Even if that is true, and the statement could I think be refuted, I still maintain that the best way to teach a child to love poetry is to start him on Longfellow.

My mother had a marvellous memory for poetry and used to repeat ballads to us. As far back as I can remember, somewhere about three and a half, I knew Sir William Hunter's translation of 'Runjit Dehu' and Sir Alfred Lyall's 'Old Pindari'. I fancy nobody reads Sir Alfred Lyall now, but he has crystallized India in his one short volume of poems, as no other writer has done. And the verse is fine and stirring. We learnt Macaulay too, chunks of him, and I used to shiver with delicious terror over,

> 'A woman fair and stately
> But pale as are the dead
> All through the long night watches
> Sat spinning by his bed.'

and

> 'The trees beneath whose shadow
> The ghastly priest doth reign,
> The priest who slew the slayer
> And shall himself be slain.'

And

> 'April's ivory moonlight,
> Under the chestnut trees'

seemed to me one of the loveliest phrases ever written. Poor children of to-day, who are told that Macaulay is a rotten Early Victorian, and whose sense of pity and terror is fed by Edgar Wallace and Sexton Blake!

A VICTORIAN CHILDHOOD

When I was nine I wrote my first poem, which I reproduce, not because it was any different from the poems most little girls and boys with literary parents write, but because it is an answer to the assertion many people make nowadays, that children have only in this generation begun to write poetry and paint pictures for their own amusement.

> 'Through the glades of life we pass,
> Never stopping, never,
> Death though always comes at last
> And we all shall sever.
>
> 'And when we shall part at last
> And we all shall sever,
> We shall never meet again,
> Never, never, never.'

At the instance of my nursery-maid I subsequently altered the last two lines to

> 'We shall some day meet again
> In the heaven yonder.'

But the original version was the true one. I was very proud of this effusion and showed it round the house.

It was about this time that my father became aware of me. His children bored him rather, and my early recollection is of a red-bearded man with very bright eyes who always said, 'Vanish, vanish', whenever any of us came into the room, so that we fled like hares when we heard him coming. But for some reason I had learnt a poem of Matthew Arnold's and my mother told me to repeat it to him. He was pleased and after this we became great friends and I was with him constantly in his beautiful purple study at York House. For by this time we had left Knebworth and moved to a fine old Jacobean house next door to the church at Twickenham, which had been built by Clarendon on the remains of an older house, and in which Queen Anne and Queen Mary her sister were born. Queen Anne's room is still there. This was haunted too, as Knebworth had been, but not nearly so seriously.

My father, Mountstuart Grant Duff, began his Diary in 1847, though he only published the part beginning in 1851. He was peculiarly fitted to make a record as he made a point of knowing all the men and women most worth knowing in Europe. Unfortunately he was also a very modest person and could never believe that anything about himself would interest anybody. So his Diary,

A VICTORIAN CHILDHOOD

though packed with information and interesting comments on people, and public affairs, does not give any impression of what a very lovable and interesting person he was himself. Full of humour, with an immense sense of drama and of picturesque happenings, had he let himself go more he would have produced one of the finest diaries existing. But he never said ill-natured things and, though he had a quick temper and could turn and rend the philistine on occasions, he never bore malice. But he did not suffer fools gladly, and still less foolesses. Several times it has been my lot to remodel a large dinner party in ten minutes, just as people were arriving, because my father absolutely refused to sit next a woman who bored him.

He was very devoted to Scotland and I do not think would have sold his family place, Eden, had not my mother disliked that country. She was a typical Englishwoman, and the bleak Scots landscape appalled her. It *is* very dour if you don't happen to have the feel of it in your blood. When they bought York House, Twickenham was still a village within easy drive of London even with horses. And it suited my mother especially, who, though she loved a garden, had no feeling for wild nature. My father bought it from the Comte de Paris who had lived there for many years. The Duc d'Aumale had a house next door and the Duc d'Orleans inhabited Orleans House also quite close. There was an underground passage uniting the properties which was afterwards bricked up and where we as children kept pet stag-beetles. My father resold York House in 1896 to the then Duc d'Orleans, the son of the Comte de Paris, who afterwards sold it to Sir Ratan Tata. It is now used as a municipal building.

My father never treated me the least as a child, but simply as a companion rather younger than himself. He made me say 'Calais Sands', the poem that first called his attention to me, to Matthew Arnold, who came very often. I used to sit on his knee and repeat his own poems to him. I remember Lord Houghton too, and how much I liked his poetry and how afraid I was of his enormous teeth. I wonder how many people nowadays know 'Why should a man raise stone and wood between him and the sky' and 'Strangers Yet'? I was also devoted to a book called *Medusa and other Poems,* by some woman. I once was made to say Hymns to Lord Napier of Magdala, who was very pious and very alarming.

I was the only person who my father's collie, Guard, who inhabited the library, did not resent. He started by flying at me and scaring me badly, seizing my arm and shaking it, but after that we became comrades and I was allowed in and out of the room as much and as often as I liked. The grey cockatoo, Cocky, also became intimate and would sit on my finger. He never made friends with my mother or any one except my father and me and would bite the rest of the household savagely if they dared to presume.

One of the things I remember most clearly before we left York House was staying, when I was about nine and soon before his death, with W. R. Greg and his wife at Park Lodge, Wimbledon. Mr. and Mrs. Greg had always been a feature in our lives as they came to the house very often. This was my first visit except to my grandmother and I felt very uplifted as I was driven over alone in solitary grandeur. I had a room to myself and there was a great medlar-tree in the garden and Walter, a quiet little boy with large eyes, was very kind to me. Mrs. Greg gave me a book called *The Necklace of Princess Fiorimonde*, by Mary de Morgan, which has remained one of my favourite books. It was illustrated by Walter Crane and round the wall of Walter's nursery there were pictures from Walter Crane's illustrations, now alas unobtainable. This is the first time I remember realizing the beauty of human form in art, and from that moment I used to try to dress myself and my small sister and brother, so as to make us look like Walter Crane pictures. We must have looked like nothing on earth, but I remember my great happiness was to walk slowly up and down in an old pale-blue lining begged from my mother's maid, in which garment I pretended to be a Princess, and in which I thought of course that I looked very beautiful. I also tried to make gardens and we used to play gardens after we had been tucked up for the night. The squares of the nursery carpet were beds and the border round it was the lawn and we used to water them with the nursery jug. Miss Schübnall constantly found the carpet wet and could not make it out, until one unhappy day when she came in during the operation and I was terribly punished.

W. R. Greg was supposed by people of his generation to have been the inspiration for Rochester in Charlotte Brontë's *Jane Eyre*. He married as his second wife, Julia, one of the six daughters of James Wilson, Secretary to the Board of Control in Lord John Russell's Government, and founder of the *Economist*. Wilson was sent out to India after the Mutiny to try and put some sort of order into the money affairs of that country and was responsible for the first railway lines laid down. In eight months he had established a stable financial system, but the effort cost him his life. Two of his sons-in-law, W. R. Greg and Walter Bagehot, were most brilliant and charming men, and his grand-daughter, Lady Colefax, has inherited a great deal of her grandfather's ability.

W. R. Greg was a great deal older than his wife, and when I knew him he was already a white-haired man with beetling brows hanging over piercing eyes. I was very fond of him and he was always charming to me, and she was one of my dearest friends until she died, though her sister

Emilie Barrington, who wrote a first-rate life of her gifted father, entitled *The Servant of All*, was an even more intimate friend. She, thank God, is still with us as I write. I did not know of course that Mr. Greg was supposed to be Rochester till years afterwards. *Jane Eyre* was the first novel I ever read, at ten years old. I cannot imagine how I got hold of it, but I used to hide myself and read it and I was terribly frightened by the episode of the mad woman tearing the wedding veil. Some weeks later my mother and Miss Caroline Erskine were discussing the work and I cheerfully put in my oar and said how interesting I found it. Miss Erskine nearly fainted with shock and turned on my poor mother saying, 'Julia, how can you let the child read that book?' My mother's horror equalled Miss Erskine's, she had of course had nothing to do with it. My next novel was *Dombey and Son* and then I read *Vanity Fair*. These grown-up novels enchanted me, but on the other hand I adored *Alice in Wonderland* and *Alice Through the Looking-Glass* and thought them extraordinarily funny. I used sometimes to try and read *Punch* and wondered why it amused people.

When I was about ten Adrian was not very well at school and it was decided that it would be better for him to be at home for a bit, and a tutor was procured called Dr. Borns, a very clever man with a distinguished mind, who remained a great friend till he died last year

It was about this time that I had my first psychic experience and I have never understood it. Miss Schübnall always locked the door into the schoolroom which was at one end of the night nursery, before she went to bed. One evening she was locking it as usual and I distinctly saw a little pink and white pig sniffing at her skirts. The pig was so real that I sat up in bed and said, 'Oh, Fräulein! sieh das Schweinchen.' Fräulein only retorted, 'Was um Gotteswillen schwatzest Du da, Es giebt hier kein Schweinchen.' But I saw the pig quite distinctly for a few moments after she had spoken and then it disappeared. Another day I was sitting in bed with Fräulein snoring loudly near me, when I saw a darling little kitten in the moonlight by the window. It never struck me that it was not a real kitten and I got up to try and take it into my bed. I tried to put my hands on it and they went together. I was very much surprised and went back to my pillow. There again was the kitten. I tried again, but this time Fräulein woke up and shouted at me. I suppose there is no reason why there should not be ghosts of animals as much as ghosts of people. I cannot understand these two psychic experiences and there was no physical cause why I should think I saw them, for I was not in the least neurotic or nervous.

At York House an immense number of people came to stay with my father and mother. Some of them we merely saw for a few minutes. Children are brought down to be stared at by inquiring friends and then sent back to the nursery. The Mallets and the Lubbocks were the ones I recollect best. The four Mallet boys were all schoolfellows of my brothers and delightful boys they were, and their father Sir Louis I always remember with affection, though he was not the least a man to attract children. Lady Mallet was a most kind woman, but I never could bear her, simply because in George MacDonald's *Fairy Tales* the giantess in one illustration was rather like Lady Mallet, and I always believed that she was quite up to eating small children. I never much liked being left alone with her. She was really a most amiable woman. I remember adoring Mrs. Augustus Craven, and was once as a great treat told to take her for a walk. She wanted very much to go to Ham House which was just opposite, but I honestly preferred the road along the canal towards Kneller Hall, where one could find certain wild flowers, and poor Mrs. Craven was taken over stile after stile, along the black canal, I firmly believing that she was having a delightful time. She arrived home in tatters and I was very much scolded, though I had sincerely done my best, thinking that that was the nicest walk in the neighbourhood. I remember Mr. Gladstone coming to stay and taking me on his knee and kissing me. I did not like old gentlemen and he was no exception to the rule. Another person whose scrubby face I particularly disliked was Professor Tyndall who sometimes came to the house. I remember a charming Jew whom we were very fond of, Leonard Montefiore, whose early death my father always deplored. He was a gifted man and clever with children.

One day the Crown Princess Frederick,

afterwards Empress of Germany, came to tea at York House. She gave my sister Dot, who was her godchild, a book called *Naseweis und Däumelinchen* which became a nursery classic. She kissed me and was very charming to all of us children. She always was good to my father and I fancy it is an open secret that she wanted him to be ambassador at Berlin. History might have been very different had she had her way.

My only boy friend was Bertrand Russell, who with his grandmother old Lady Russell, Lord John's widow, lived at Pembroke Lodge, in Richmond Park. Bertie and I were great allies and I had an immense secret admiration for his beautiful and gifted elder brother Frank. Frank, I am sorry to say, sympathized with my brother's point of view about little girls and used to tie me up to trees by my hair. But Bertie, a solemn little boy in a blue velvet suit with an equally solemn governess, was always kind, and I greatly enjoyed going to tea at Pembroke Lodge. But even as a child I realized what an unsuitable place it was for children to be brought up in. Lady Russell always spoke in hushed tones and Lady Agatha always wore a white shawl and looked down-trodden. Rollo Russell never spoke at all. He gave one a handshake that nearly broke all the bones of one's fingers, but was quite friendly. They all drifted in and out of the rooms like ghosts and no one ever seemed to be hungry. It was a curious bringing up for two young and extraordinarily gifted boys.

The only girl friends I had of my own age were both called Maud. Maud Walpole, daughter of Mr., afterwards Sir, Spencer and Lady Walpole, who were like a second mother and father to me, and Maud Griffiths, now Mrs. Alford. Maud Walpole married Frank Holland and I have remained friends with both of them. Amongst grown-ups I remember Mr. Kinglake and Sir James Lacaita vaguely, and Sir James Hudson distinctly. I came in one day just as lunch was finishing and Sir James Hudson, with delightful courtesy, got up and kissed my hand. It was at Knebworth and I must have been about six at the time, but I never forgot the incident. My father told me afterwards who the gentleman was who had so honoured me.

My godmother, Lady Henley, was a great feature in my life. She was a superbly handsome woman of the Rubens type, with gold red hair and a dazzling white skin, a warm-hearted, amusing delightful creature, who always treated me exactly like her own child. She had lost her little girl of my age and I think in a small way I took her place. I was named after this godmother Clara, Annabel after my grandmother whose name was Hannah, and Caroline after Miss Caroline Erskine, a great friend of my mother. But no one ever called me anything but Tiny. I weighed only three and a half pounds when I was born, which accounts for the nickname. And I was only addressed as Clara when I had been naughty, hence I suppose my horror of the name. When I considered myself too old to be called Tiny I signed myself Annabel, but Tiny persists.

My godfather was Lord de Tabley the poet, a romantic figure whom I remember vaguely as a child, though much more distinctly later on, a shy charming scholarly man with a delightful smile and a gift for saying witty and graceful things. One day when I was about twenty and had just published my first poem, he came in carrying a small book and said, 'My dear, as we are both in the same line I thought you would like this.' It was his last book of verse.

Other people I recall are Professors Huxley and Owen, Mr. and Mrs. Green the historians, and Dr. Jowett who had christened me as a baby. But more intimate memories are connected with Sir Charles Dilke and Henry Smith and George von Bunsen. No one ever understood children like Sir Charles Dilke, and Henry Smith had the lovableness of a child himself. Both used constantly to come to the schoolroom.

Sir Charles Dilke and Mrs. Mark Pattison, whom he subsequently married, used to come and stay very often. I did not like her, I do not think any child ever did. She was very brilliant but had a certain want of sincerity. I was always very annoyed because Sir Charles Dilke very naturally wanted to talk to her when I wanted him to play with me, and there was no love lost between us. It is very difficult to say what made Henry Smith, Jupiter Smith as he was called at Oxford, so attaching. He was very witty, but as a child I could not know this, for children do not in the least understand wit, but I know we hailed his visits with delight and he used to come and play bears with us. I was very sorry when I heard, when still a schoolgirl, that he was dead. My father could never speak of him, even to the end of his life, without his voice breaking. He had a picture of him on an easel in his library which he always kept locked up, but I have often found him standing staring at it when I came in unexpectedly, and then he would close the doors hastily.

Very distinctly I remember Baron Malortie and his beautiful wife coming to stay. She was quite exquisite and children are very sensitive to beauty. For years I kept a photograph of her.

It was before I was ten, though I do not quite remember when, that I was taken to my first dramatic entertainment. It was organized by Mrs. Labouchere, the wife of the great journalist, and took place at Twickenham Town Hall. I forget what the play was, I think it was *The Belles Stratagem* or something like that, but I can still see with startling clearness a young girl who acted with Mrs. Labouchere and whose beauty drove all the men of the party perfectly wild. Herbert Gladstone was staying with us at the time and I do not know

A VICTORIAN CHILDHOOD

which was the most lost in admiration, he or my father. The girl was Lily Langtry and it was her first appearance on the boards. Small wonder that she turned our heads.

We all disliked York House very much as children, though I became fond of it later on. It was far less attractive than either Hampden or Knebworth had been and the boys regretted Scotland terribly. I wish my mother had not so hated Scotland and that we could have been brought up there, but both she and my father were ambitious people and wanted to give political parties and York House suited their purpose. The house and garden were very beautiful and neither of them cared particularly about the country though they were fond of flowers. I disliked York House less than the boys who found very little to do except go on the river, which they did all day and every day. This was my great solace later, but I was not allowed to go out alone until I was twenty.

We were a certain amount in London, though I cannot say that I remember it clearly. But I have never forgotten the blue-grey of the park on winter afternoons, and the black trees standing out from the sunset. Whenever I hear a muffin-man I shut my eyes and see the balls of the plane-trees hanging against the sky. I wanted one of those balls more than anything on earth and I never found one till I was too old to care.

I remember expeditions to the Round Pond and saving pennies for balloons and how I always hated Punch and Judy shows. I had no sense of humour, and to see people knocked about and killed, or people falling down with trays of china and smashing looking-glasses has never amused me, as it does those blessed with that priceless gift.

We scarcely ever went to parties, but I remember one at Judge, then Mr. Snagge's, at which both Adrian and I distinguished ourselves. Adrian by saying pleasantly to his host on being ushered into the drawing-room, 'I don't like this drawing-room, ours at home is prettier,' and I by insisting on singing a hymn. It was represented to me that it was not the moment, but I was pious and not to be deterred. So I sang a hymn very loudly to an embarrassed crowd of various ages and was only stopped by an ice. On another occasion we were sent with Mrs. French to see the Lord Mayor's Show from

Sir Erskine May's house, and Mrs. French asked my mother where we should lunch. 'Oh, I expect there will be some sort of scratch lunch,' said my mother. So when greeted by Lady May I announced politely, 'We've come to have some kind of scratch lunch.' These are the only parties I remember when I was quite small. Children went to few in those days and I only recall one pantomime before I was ten. It must have been *Cinderella* for there were large rats which frightened me.

I remember one delightful week in London as the guest of old Mr. Childers, minister for Ireland, in Mr. Gladstone's third government. His daughters, Louise, later Mrs. Simeon, and Millie, were both very kind, and it was during this stay that I found an earwig in Queen's Gate Gardens, and Kate Thring, Lord Thring's daughter, explained to me what it was. It filled me with genuine horror, which I have never forgotten, and I am so glad I am not a clergyman, as these insects are said to prefer the ears of divines.

When I was ten and a half we were sent to the New Forest for a change of air. Maud Walpole and her father and mother were staying at the same hotel, the White Hart, near Lyndhurst. I had never seen a forest before and adored the trees and the long vistas of grass through them, in those days unspoilt by trippers. Maud and I invented a beautiful game called Pigs which we played with passion. It is a curious game, for I never found *any one* at any age who did not like playing it. I have set shooting parties to play it and they became as absorbed as the children. Each person chooses a sty and makes it comfortable and safe. Sticks or stones round the sty make it impregnable. But if there is the smallest loophole the wolf may get in. All day the pigs circulate freely in the forest. But any time after the clock strikes eight there is danger and the wolf may turn up suddenly. The game can be varied infinitely. If you play with werepigs, your friend and companion may be a werepig in disguise and rend you. The greatest compliment I was ever paid was when my two eldest children were about ten and eight. We were playing pigs and my girl Konradin suddenly in a fit of enthusiasm flung her arms round me and said in French, which we always talked, 'Oh, Mummum, when we are playing pigs,

I forget that you are my Mummum and I think that you are another child.' I was delighted and said to Fritzl, 'I do hope you feel that too?'—'No,' said Fritzl with a faraway look in his eyes, 'when you play pigs I forget that you are a person and I think that you really *are* a pig!' It sounds so much worse in French, 'Oh, Maman, quand tu joues, joublie que tu es une personne. Je pense que tu es *vraiment* un cochon!' Le Mot!

Shortly after we returned from the New Forest I noticed, as children do, that my mother and father were very excited about something, and there was a great deal of coming and going and telegrams and important-looking people arrived to see my father. About a week after that my mother called me and told me that we were going to India. When I had recovered my breath I asked, 'And are the boys coming too?' and my mother said, 'No, I am afraid not.' I burst into tears and my mother kissed me because she thought it showed such nice feeling. It was really overwhelming relief, the thought that there would be no holidays in which I should be bullied and tormented was too much for me.

After that life was one delirious dream. We had always been very simply dressed, partly because with such a large family my parents were not rich, and partly because my mother thought it better to dress children in the plainest clothes. Now a whole trousseau was procured for Dot and me. Everybody gave us parting presents and all were excited at our change of fortune.

We had a big afternoon dance to bid farewell to our friends, and at this I heard Strauss Waltzes for the first time and went mad, as every one must, over the Blue Danube. Mrs. St. Loe Strachey, then Miss Simpson, was at that dance, a handsome girl of sixteen, and so were the Huxley girls and all the Lubbocks and a Mr. Townshend Griffin who talked to me as if I was grown up, an unforgettable episode.

I remember going to stay with my grandmother for the last time and how sad she seemed. I was really fond of her, but I had not the slightest idea that I should never see her again. Children have no sense of age and I did not realize that she was a very old woman. She kissed me tenderly and told me not to forget her, and the servants too seemed moved when I went away. I

LADY GRANT DUFF AND ANNABEL JACKSON
BETWEEN THE AGES OF 10-11

never saw her again after the 5th of October when she came to Tilbury to say good-bye on board the *Rome* in which we sailed for India.

Fräulein Schübnall was left behind, a great mistake I think, and substituted for her was Mademoiselle Vuillamet, who, poor thing, was not born to be an educationalist. I suffer from real remorse when I think how badly we all treated her and how unkind we were. I suppose in the depths of my heart I was getting my own back on Mademoiselle Reinking and Nurse Maunder, but we certainly made her life a burden and she was a harmless inoffensive person, but she did not wash and that to the childish mind, however averse to washing the young may be themselves, is a dreadful sin. I happened to be a clean child, so was particularly down on her grubbiness. She only stayed about six months, and then was succeeded by Miss Moxon, whom we were also not very nice to. In fact looking back I think I must have been thoroughly odious for the next three years.

As the vessel moved off I saw my grandmother, very pale, leaning over the rail and my three brothers with her. Every one was sobbing and that heartbreaking cheer went up which accompanies the departure of a ship. I sobbed too. At the last moment I remembered all that Adrian had been to me and I wished that he was coming too.

CHAPTER IV

AS we steamed down the river, a big heavy man with two daughters came up and introduced himself as the Government House doctor, Dr. Mackenzie, and two aides-de-camp, Captain Cavendish and Captain Gordon, also greeted us. We explored the ship and played hide and seek along the little narrow passages and after a few days we were in summer and the phosphorescent water lashed against the boat's keel.

Every incident of the voyage out was a delight—Malta with its palaces, where we spent a day, Suez and Port Said with their donkey rides and queer mixed people. Aden seemed to me very beautiful, though everybody told me it was a horrid place. And at last we came to Bombay, and the wonder of an Indian town. In those days India was not English as it is now, it was scarcely touched by Western civilization and there were exquisite things to be bought in the bazaars, and romance all round. My father was met by the Governor at Bombay and went straight to Government House, but the nursery party were sent off to Madras by the night train, and had a most delightful two days watching all the things that were to be seen from the carriage windows and not in the least minding the heat, which reduced the nurse Bachelor and the maid Drysdale to a state of soporific indignation. Bachelor was always cross. I never knew her pleased with anything and I have never been able to understand how my mother put up with her, but she was devoted to her and kept her first as our nurse and then as her maid for thirty years.

At Bombay some of the old soldiers who had served under my grandfather in the Mahratta War came to greet my father. In those days, before we had ruined our prestige in India by letting men go out there who were not gentlemen, and were rude to the natives, there was a friendly feeling between Indians and Englishmen and these old men remembered my grandfather with affection.

We children arrived in Madras early one morning and were met by a third aide-de-camp, a most beautiful human being, and a charming person, Arthur Bagot, to whom I owe more than most people owe each other. He and I made friends at once. First he was a big brother for many years and then my devoted friend until he died. He was good all through and I have never known him say a mean or cowardly thing. Magnificently good-looking, a perfect horseman, a wonderful dancer and a first-rate shot, to me he was for all the world like some one out of a fairy-tale. He took us from the station to Government House and we were ushered into an enormous room where about twenty-five people were breakfasting. I was most terribly shy, nearly frightened to death, and of course swaggered in consequence, as children do. I remember sitting between a man called Lord Dalhousie and another man called Lord Abercrombie who fed me and asked me endless questions. I was very thankful when we were taken off to bed to sleep off the effects of our journey in a great cool room under mosquito curtains.

After a long rest we went for a drive in one of the State carriages with splendid horses and scarlet liveries. We were very carefully dressed and I remember my surprise at being dressed up this way to go for

A VICTORIAN CHILDHOOD

a simple drive. We drove along the sea front past Marine Villa, where Etta and Maud Mackenzie had gone to live in a delightful domicile. We saw numbers of Anglo-Indians taking the air much as people do in England in Hyde Park, meeting friends and gossiping. We were very bored and the next day we were allowed to go for a walk in the Park instead, and I shall never forget the enchantment of it. There was a round pool fringed with coconut palms, with kingfishers flying in and out everywhere and great butterflies nearly as big as the kingfishers, sailing about. There were herds of little black deer so small they were not much bigger than a fox terrier, and beautiful brown women with great brass pots on their heads, going down to fetch water. Everywhere there were the loveliest flowers and great crimson bushes or flowering trees, but it was not until I got to Guindy that I realized the wonders of India. Guindy is a palace built as a sort of country residence for the Governor some way out of Madras, but near enough to the sea for us children to go down to it very often. The grounds had been very carefully planned and were full of the most exquisite flowers. There were acres of divine gardens and outside were the paddy fields and a small miniature racecourse where one could get a good gallop in the early morning.

Whilst he was there my father had all the Guindy flowers painted by a native artist. He used to come every morning, a simple little man, almost naked, who just sat and painted. But he had the great old Indian tradition and these pictures are now my most cherished possession. I do not even know his name.

Two beautiful Arab ponies were bought for Hampden and me, one called Omar and one called Ali. Ali was the most beautiful and was given to me. The first day I rode him he bucked me off. I was put up again another day and he bucked me off again, so he was sold and I was given Omar and another pony was bought for Hampden.

By this time I had completely lost my nerve and was so abjectly terrified that my rides were the one bleak spot in an otherwise perfect and happy life. I still remember the terror of dressing for those rides. We had a coachman called James Tagg whom we had brought out from England with us, who had married a housemaid.

A VICTORIAN CHILDHOOD

He was a clever and an amusing man, but he had many faults. However he taught us to ride and jump, also to saddle and bridle a horse, and to mount and dismount without any help; all most useful accomplishments, and which every one ought to learn as young as possible.

There were a hundred horses in the stables, each with its syce, grasscutter and woman to boil its 'dal', a kind of lentil. The stables were kept like a drawing-room and the horses polished with the naked hand. I never saw a groom in our stables rough with a horse, though James Tagg was rough enough and gave them a bad example. When I got my nerve back I practically had the run of the riding stables and as my hands were good, the staff let me ride their mounts.

There were a hundred servants in the house, efficient and attentive and capable, and then of course there were the numberless boys belonging to the staff and the gardeners and so on, outside. The indoor servants or peons were picturesquely dressed in long flowing robes with gold and red or red turbans according to rank. Some of the superior servants wore only gold and red.

JAMES GRANT DUFF OF EDEN

Everything moved on oiled wheels, especially when Colonel Kenney Herbert the great cook, and most delightful person, became Military Secretary. He was a first-rate actor as well as a perfect housewife, and his daughter and I were fast friends.

I remember a performance of *Patience* organized by Colonel Kenney Herbert, which was far, far better than any Savoy performance I ever saw. Of course he had an enormous choice, with the whole of Madras society to pick from, so small wonder that the cast was first-rate.

I had been taught to ride at three and a half at Hampden, as I have already said. At Knebworth I remember James Tagg putting me on a pony and then lunging it. I was so terribly frightened that when it was over I picked up the tail of my long habit and walked straight into the library where my father was sitting and said, 'I have had a terwibble nervous sock and will never wide again.' My father very sensibly forbade my being put on a horse and I did not ride again until I was eight and then I asked to, because a friend had a pony. James Tagg took me out in Richmond Park and I rode fearlessly for a year and a half on a pony called Pixie, a Shetland. But the two falls off Ali broke my nerve and I did not get it back again for six months.

It was at Government House, Madras, that we had our tree that first Christmas in India, when I was eleven. It was an orange-tree and was covered with little yellow balls and presents and was quite enchanting. I remember how strangely happy I was that evening and how I suddenly realized how much Captain Gordon meant to me.

He was one of those men with whom all women fall in love, and no one particularly knows why. He was good-looking—but no better-looking than many men in that age of tall finely made men—with dark hair, a slightly reddish moustache, an aquiline nose and clear skin. He had a delightful baritone voice and was really musical, and he danced and rode and shot and played polo well. But in my youth these accomplishments were expected of any soldier. He was not nearly as handsome as Captain Arthur Bagot, though a cleverer man. But there was no doubt about his charm for women; it was universally admitted.

Few people know how many children fall in love and what agonies they suffer. The

A VICTORIAN CHILDHOOD

day I was eleven I became aware of my absorption in Captain Gordon, but for some time I did not really understand what had happened. I just adored him and wanted to be with him always, and then suddenly came the comprehension, 'This is what people mean when they say they are in love.' The inevitable happened and he fell in love with me and for six months more our idyll endured, unsuspected by any one, carefully protected by the Indian servants with their genius for intrigue, a beautiful thing, however foolish it may have been on my part and wrong on his. Looking back—it is nearly fifty years ago—I marvel at the passion a child could feel. . . . Passion undisturbed by the faintest lust. I had not the remotest idea what sex love meant and I cannot be grateful enough that this unique experience was given me. I see now that my lover must have suffered a good deal. Sometimes when he had held me in his arms and kissed me blind, he would suddenly say, 'Run away, quick, quick,' and I used to tear off wondering and very much hurt, and noticing as I went that his face was working horribly and very white. When I was a woman I looked back and understood. The supreme instinct that comes to women from their cradles onward came to me and I became so fine an actress that no one except Arthur Bagot and the native servants ever guessed. My mother was naturally unobservant and my father lived his own life and rarely saw us together. My governess could not conceive the possibility of a grown-up man falling in love with a child and my small brother and sister and the two Mackenzie girls never thought about anything at all.

To Captain Gordon I owe a great deal of my love of music. He sang me Schubert and Schumann and was always telling me that nothing in life mattered like music. In his last letter to me before he went away he said, 'Keep up your music, whatever else you do or do not do, take trouble over it. You will find it a solace and a consolation when everything else leaves you and disappoints you.' He used to read me the Epic of Hades, and Byron, and Keats and Heine in his beautiful grave voice. He taught me to see effects of cloud and shadow over the hills, and as he was passionately fond of flowers, I was always trying to find new ones and arrange them in his room. I owe him a great deal, though he broke my heart.

I have always been like a man—my love-affairs have not touched the rest of my life. And this absorbing first passion of mine, though it coloured every moment when I was alone, did not prevent my rushing about with other children and amusing myself in various ways when I could not be with my lover. When Captain Gordon left the hills in November we had a heart-breaking parting and I cried myself sick. But I thought he would be back in three months. However, when he got to the plains Arthur Bagot went to him and said, 'If you do not arrange to change into another regiment and leave the staff I shall go to His Excellency.' I only knew this later in life. When I got the news that he was not coming back I nearly went out of my mind. I used to wander over the hills, hiding in the woods and sobbing my heart out. And then I would wash my eyes in a mountain stream and go back in high spirits. No one ever had any conception of what it meant, and when my mother spoke to me about it a year or two later, I merely said, 'Oh yes, I was very fond of him, but not really as fond as I am of Arthur Bagot.' And there the matter ended. Years after I met him again when I was eighteen and I asked him, 'How could you have made love to me like that?' He answered, 'God forgive me, I was so madly in love with you that I did not know what I was doing.' That was the last time I spoke to him. He married soon after, a woman much older than himself. Long years later I sat opposite to him at a big dinner-party but he went away directly the meal was over and we did not speak to each other again. And then he died.

I am always glad that I had the one overwhelming experience which falls to so few women, very young. It gave me a standard to measure other men by. Probably had I not fallen in love as a child I should have fallen in love later and married the wrong man. As it was my marriage was a supreme success, because I knew that 'Love' alone was not a sufficiently strong foundation to build marriage on. Had I married Captain Gordon it would have been disastrous.

At Guindy we discovered where the French cook kept the turtles that were to be devoured when there was a banquet and we used to go out and cut the string which was tied to the animals' legs, so that they got away. The poor cook was naturally very angry and an enmity began between us which was exploited in every possible way, annoying him terribly, poor man. As he had always been very kind and made us sweets, this was unpardonable.

The only drawback against English children being in India is that they have much too much power over servants and it is very bad for small children to exercise power. I do not think the climate in many places can harm them if they are carefully fed on vegetables and not stuffed with meat and other horrors. My father tried to get us taught Botany by an Eurasian, but we heard people say it was a mistake for the Governor to do this and were very rude to the clever man who came to teach us, so these lessons had to be given up.

My father and mother improved the music at Guindy by making a certain Monsieur Stradiot the leader of the band. Stradiot was a man of genius and the music was really first-rate as long as my people remained in India.

My mother got up a ladies' orchestra, with the help of a Dr. Maclean, and a scribbling club for amateurs to write and have their work criticized. She also started

A VICTORIAN CHILDHOOD

a sketching club and she did an immense amount for the schools and all philanthropic organizations in Madras.

I have always heard that my father was a very good Governor. He improved the Forestry Department very much and he visited and went into the grievances of every part of his domain. The other day an old Indian told me that a common saying after he left was, 'We had a Duff and now we have a Duffer,' referring to his successor. I remember as a small child hearing my father say that India would be lost by the fact that we were no longer sending out the same class of men to govern her and to take part in the various services. I think that subsequent events have proved how very wise he was. Half the trouble in India is caused by the third-rate men and women who go out there simply to have a good time and who talk about 'Dirty Natives' and who never attempt to understand the culture that they have come into. When one thinks of the average Anglo-Indian bungalow, as it was in my time, full of the vulgarest kind of European stuff and tenanted by women who cared for nothing but self-indulgence and amusing themselves, one can scarcely wonder at the cynical disbelief the native has in the reality of European civilization. On the other hand, there are wonderful men who have given their lives for the country of their adoption and who care more about India than the Indians themselves. But in India as in England the Englishman's lust of pleasure has been his undoing.

From Guindy we moved to Ootacamund about the first of March. My mother was near her confinement and it was supposed to be better for the children to be moved away from the heat. We had never seen the mountains before and the drive up from Mettapoliam would have been a joy had we not been so terribly frightened in the tongas. The little ponies dashed along up almost perpendicular roads and constantly slipped back, every now and then falling, with their incompetent drivers shrieking at them from behind. We were very tired and were put to bed as soon as we got to Ootacamund, but the next morning waking to the great mountains was an experience I shall never forget. There were eucalyptus woods carpeted with white violets and tiny streams meandering along on every side, there were sholas of great aboriginal trees full of jasmine and every kind of flower and there were thickets of wattle covered with little yellow balls smelling as no mimosa smells on the corner of a London street. There were belladonna and arum lilies and little wild narcissus growing everywhere, and every now and then the great rare Nilgeri lily.

Every one was occupied with my mother and the new baby, which was born on the twelfth of March and we were practically left alone and Hampden and I explored the marvellous country in complete happiness. I do not remember many lessons at that moment. It was at that time that Mademoiselle Vuillamet left and in the interim we were sent to a French convent, looked after by the most delightful set of nuns I have come across, most of them women of good family, and one of them one of the most beautiful creatures I have seen. Mère Antoine was very tall and very pale with a few little freckles and gold eyebrows and eyelashes. She was so beautiful that I never could think of anything at all except her face when she was in the room. And I remember being rebuked by Soeur François de Sales for staring at her and I answered that she was so beautiful I could not help it. She explained to me that external beauty was a wile of the Devil himself and that it did not make any difference to us or to our natures. In God's eyes it might quite possibly be ugly. I did not dare contradict her, but I knew her to be wrong.

Mademoiselle Vuillamet with all her faults had made us talk French and I could speak it quite easily. And I was given Roche's anthology and allowed to choose my own poems. I was doubtless attracted by the fact that I found a rhyme easier to remember than blank verse, but it remains to my credit that I chose 'Le Lac' and 'Ta Douleur du Perrier' and 'Les Roses de Saadi' myself. I had also found out much English poetry unassisted and my favourite poems before I was twelve were Keats' 'St. Agnes Eve' and the 'Ancient Mariner', discovered in a lovely old illustrated book.

We used to ride to the Convent in the early morning and lunch there, then we got back in the evening. We went for about six weeks of that year and for longer the year after. I used to love going to Benediction, the service that first showed me what worship meant. We had our meals in the parlour; pears in syrup and light red French wine and gruyère cheese and omelettes for lunch. Nothing has ever tasted so good.

My first experience of acting was at the Convent rather later on. The nuns needed money and one of the sisters wrote a play about the French Revolution, *Marie de Rieux*. It was an incident in the life of her own forebears and the story was of a twin sister who was smuggled into prison and dies impersonating her brother to save the line. It was an excellent play and at the first full rehearsal all were so moved that actors and managers were in tears and the rehearsal had to be stopped. I was Marie de Rieux and Dolly Soutar, a most brilliant child, was my brother. We acted for a week and made a lot of money besides the immense pleasure of seeing our audience mopping their eyes night after night. As a curtain raiser we acted a play of Madame de Ségur called *Le Chat parti, les Souris dansent*, in French. I felt terribly important riding over to the Convent every morning with powdered hair and being given *syrop de fleurs d'oranger* to clear my throat. The nun who coached me, Mother Sebastian,

A VICTORIAN CHILDHOOD

was a very able old lady and taught me no end about acting in the short time. She also taught me heraldry and I wish I had kept up that fascinating study.

CHAPTER V

I WAS always nervous on horseback and did not really like it. One day I told Captain Gordon this and he said, 'I should ask your mother to let you give it up if you are so frightened.' I was so furious that he should think me frightened that I said I would like to go hunting the next day. The staff laughed at me but the Military Secretary, Colonel Spencer, said, 'Very well, if she wants to, let her go.' My mother let me go and for the first ten minutes I was scared beyond words, but after that my blood was up and I rode all day without showing any fear at all. I used to love hunting and the jackals nearly always got away, which increased my pleasure.

How wonderful those days on the Nilgeris were. The field was never large, twenty to thirty people at the most, and they all knew each other and each other's ponies. There was the pleasant meeting in the fresh morning and then perhaps four hours' ride over the most beautiful country in the world, and real danger, for it is no light thing to gallop straight down a hillside that most people would fear to run down. One awful day the whole field went down a hill which had been pitted for cinchona-trees and one man, I think his name was Gore Langton, went literally head over heels, horse and all. Sir Frederick, afterwards Lord Roberts, the Commander-in-Chief, used to come out with his very nice girls, Edwina and Aileen, and his charming aide-de-camp, now Sir Ian Hamilton. The Roberts' family disapproved of me, a bad small child not at all properly brought up. I had a great admiration for them, but I secretly thought I had a more amusing time owing to my vices. They and their good governess, Miss Pride, were often at tea with us, for our fathers were much thrown together. But their attitude towards life was a different one to ours, and we were none of us ever the least intimate. Sir Ian, however, I have always thought a charming person and his wife equally so. My father had a great affection for him.

Sir Frederick Roberts, as he then was,

had a terror of cats, and if one was seen in the policies, every one was called in to chase the poor beast off. I, brought up to adore cats, used to think this very odd. He was a very peppery old gentleman and would get excited out hunting if things did not go to his liking.

Miss Moxon sang a great deal, not very well, and only the ballads of the day. But I admired them immensely, Virginia Gabriel, Claribel, Milton Wellings, Molloy, all very sticky and sugary. But there were more developed musicians about, Mr. Webster, Gracie Martin, and Dr. Maclean gave me a taste of better things, and I soon grew out of Milton Wellings. But I must confess to a weakness for the mellifluous sentimentality of Emile Waldteufel's waltzes which I have never quite outgrown.

All this time I was reading a great deal to my father. I would read to him from seven in the morning until nine o'clock and often for an hour in the middle of the day and then again at six. It was much too much for a child of my age, and I got very run down and the doctor told my mother that I could not possibly do lessons and read so much to my father. My father said

SIR MOUNTSTUART GRANT DUFF, SIR JOHN HANBURY WILLIAMS, AND CAPTAIN ARTHUR BAGOT

I had better give up lessons, which I did. So that all the education I got I received in father's library and I was practically his secretary. He did not like the way any of his staff read out loud and as his weak eyesight necessitated his having some one always at hand, for what he needed, I read, and amassed a curious conglomeration of knowledge. I also wrote from dictation and copied into French, English, and German, and he insisted on my learning the first four rules of Arithmetic, which he said was all any woman need ever know. His point of view may have been old-fashioned, but I have been struck in later life to find how much more accurate I, trained in this simple way, am than most of the women of my acquaintance who have been carefully taught arithmetic.

Up till eight or nine I got my sums into dreadful confusion because to me numbers always suggested individuals and had such definite personalities that I objected to the ones who did not suit being placed together. 3, for instance, was a bad little girl, 5 a boy of weak character, and I had a strong feeling that 3 would corrupt 5 if placed near him. 9 was a grown-up woman with nearly un-

A VICTORIAN CHILDHOOD

limited power but not very trustworthy and 8 a stupid servant. 7 was a man and on the whole beneficent, and 4 was a really attractive and wholesome boy. This sounds very cracky and I never mentioned it to any one till I was well over forty, and then, discussing childish things with a younger sister, I told her of this aberration. 'How odd,' she said. 'I used to do the same thing.' I do not know if it is usual for children to visualize numbers like this and I never met with any other instance of it except in the case of my sister Iseult. Like nearly all observant children, I saw faces in clouds, in the grain of wood and in the marks on ceilings. I am inclined to think that a certain school of painting is founded on this. A man sees significant form in something, it suggests an idea to his mind and he elaborates it. He then gives the result a title. It is purely a literary faculty and has nothing to do with art as practised by all the great graphic artists since the world began, men who have tried to paint what they saw and not what they thought.

We children always lunched in the dining-room and there were never less than fifteen or twenty people. I remember old Bishop Gell and his sister coming often, and Mr. Grigg and his wife, Sir Edward Grigg's parents. Then there was a delightful Colonel Martin and his two daughters, Gertrude and Gracie the musician. I also remember old Dr. Bidie, of the Forestry Department, and Mr. Pogson the astronomer and Sir William Hunter who used to tell me queer legends. He was very arresting and the sort of person children like. I used to read his books and translations of ballads and his *Old Missionary* at a very early age, and I remember his astonishment when he found out I knew Omar Khayyám by heart.

There was a family called Chamier whom I remember being always very kind. I kept up with them after I left India and used to stay with them sometimes at Cheltenham. There were a lot of very pretty Miss Tarrants who seemed very elegant to me and a lovely Miss Lonsdale. But all these people were shadows and the only ones that really mattered were Captain Bagot and Captain Gordon with whom I spent my days. Captain Bagot taught me riding, driving, dancing, how to write a decent letter, how to shake hands, how to come in and out of a room, everything which the proverbial brother is supposed to teach and which he never does. He warded off unsatisfactory acquaintances, got me out of two or three dubious love-affairs and gave me a rudimentary notion of what is meant by good form. All these things sank in and bore fruit much later. He was a most delightful companion, for when he was with children he would take the child's point of view and would perfectly understand when one wanted to gallop over hills and get off and pick flowers or even scramble in and out of a stream.

The second winter we were left alone at Ootacamund with Miss Moxon, James Tagg and his wife and a nursery-maid, whilst the rest of the establishment went down to Madras, taking Dot with them. Almost the first Sunday we were left up there, the syces went out and left the ponies tethered on the grass in front of the house, and the opportunity was too good to be missed. Hampden and I immediately scrambled on and tried to learn bare-back riding. Miss Moxon, who should have forbidden it, came out and tried too. The whole episode only lasted about ten minutes, for my horse kicked violently and flung me over his head. The pain was so sickening that for a moment I think I lost consciousness, then I got up and tried to pretend I was all right, but I finally had to go back to the house in frightful agony. Miss Moxon, realizing how foolish she had been, was naturally very anxious to make out that I was not hurt, however she presently sent for a doctor. The doctor was fifty miles away on a case and did not come till eleven o'clock at night. I shall never forget the suffering of that afternoon and evening. When he did come Miss Moxon said 'It is only a sprain, is it not?' and he said, 'Only four bones broken and I have no chloroform.' So he set me as best he could and I was put to bed. I think he mercifully sent for an opiate of some kind.

That day marked an epoch in my life. Firstly, it gave me a taste of unbearable pain, and secondly, it taught me that if you only say a thing forcefully enough, people obey you. Miss Moxon had worried me all afternoon with meaningless remarks and officiousness, and at last, desperate with pain and nerves, I said very quietly, 'Please, Miss Moxon, go straight out of the room and don't come back till the doctor comes. *Now—at once—go.*' To my intense surprise she burst into tears and went, and I registered the incident mentally.

The pain was awful for three days and then it began to get better and I was able to go round in a dressing-gown all strapped up.

Miss Moxon lost any authority she may have had after this by her folly in letting me get hurt and I suppose this was why she used to let me play cards with James Tagg and his wife and an old ruffian called Brown who was head of the tonga depôt in the neighbourhood. He was an American who had lived all his life in the worst parts of Texas and we became fast friends. He taught me a great deal about life and he also taught me to be quite a past master at whist and I was better than any old colonel by the time that winter was over. Brown, though said to be a queer character, was very amusing and had read widely; he used to borrow my books and I used to borrow his. James Tagg, who was equally queer, was also amusing. I remember once meeting a pretty lady on the road who scarcely noticed his salute when he touched his hat, and hearing him soliloquize whilst he rode behind me, 'I don't like them women as

GOVERNMENT HOUSE, OOTACAMUND

GOVERNMENT HOUSE, MADRAS

looks as if they was smelling mince pies in 'eaven.' It was such a beautiful description of the slight acknowledgement given by a certain type of English woman that I have never forgotten it.

A particular interlude that winter was the advent of a Mr. Breeks Atkinson who was a Collector in the district for some time. He was a clever interesting man and extraordinarily good to me and I used to see a lot of him as he took me for long walks.

I do not suppose that now even a child could go walking about publicly in a dressing-gown, but then the hills were so empty and silent in winter that it would not have mattered much if one had walked about in a towel.

One of the advantages of leaving England was that I was given a room of my own. Nobody who has not been a sensitive imaginative child in a large family can appreciate what that meant to me. The boredom of sleeping in a nursery constantly wakened by the baby screaming or the dog whining or the nurse snoring, can only be gauged by those who have suffered it. When we arrived in Madras I had a room to myself where I could have all my own things and where nobody ever came. It was like being in Heaven and I immediately began to collect objects which I thought beautiful for my room. We were given a rupee a week as pocket money and we used to go to the old dealer, Framjee Pestonjee, who lived at the gates of Government House and buy odds and ends with our rupees. I fancy he let us have very much what we pleased and put it down to His Excellency the Governor, but anyway we certainly got an enormous amount for our rupee, and I still have a charming old piece of Satsuma and another of Cloisonne which I picked up from him. I kept a great bowl of rose-leaves in my room which I collected fresh every morning. What happy days and nights I spent there! Wonderful Indian nights when the moon flooded everything and nobody knew that I went on the verandah and stayed watching the sleeping palms. One exciting evening when we had been to see the Muhurrum Festival I was awakened by a most fearful noise of tom-toms and fifes, and from my window I could see the procession passing along the road carrying a great silver filagree tomb, a replica of the tomb of Omar and

Ali, which was carried from the Mosque and thrown into the river. I shall never forget that wild procession with all its torches and the great silver tomb held aloft in the midst.

When we moved to Guindy I still had a room to myself and also at Ootacamund, and my instinct for decoration which had first awakened when I read the description of Little Eva's room in *Uncle Tom's Cabin* at nine years old, became a definite bias. Mrs. Beecher Stowe had an extraordinary dramatic sense and the atmosphere she contrived to put round the girl is remarkable, and it is not surprising that that pure, exquisite child's room should have affected another child deeply. So also did a very different chapter, the account of St. Clare's death, which first introduced me to the 'De Profundis'. I used to go about murmuring—

> 'Rex tremendae majestatis
> Qui salvandos salvas gratis
> Salva me, fons pietatis.
>
> . . . . .
>
> 'Recordare Jesu Pie
> Quod sum causa tuae viae
> Ne me perdas ille die.'

Years afterwards one of my children made me sing the English version six times through during an air raid! She said that it prevented her being frightened, and it did eventually put her to sleep! The grim splendour of those great words, punctuated by crashes, remains an unforgettable experience.

But to return to my instinct for decoration. My mother had a great deal of taste and always made the houses where we lived very attractive, and I expect I inherited mine from her. I remember when I was only eleven begging for an old unused closet to do up. I made my furniture out of packing-cases and so on and covered it with cheap gaudy stuff from the bazaars. I was always making gardens and I had many hidden away in the sholas round Government House. Nowadays if a child showed such marked tendencies to create it would be given every opportunity to learn and develop its taste, but nobody took any notice of these interests of mine, they merely said, 'She seems to be able to amuse herself alone all right.' With no brothers to bother me, I could create little houses everywhere, and did so and lived a strange happy life of my

A VICTORIAN CHILDHOOD

own varied by altercations with my governess with whom I was not on good terms. She thought me a very eccentric child, small blame to her, poor woman. She had amazingly bad taste in literature and allowed me to read all the novels of Mrs. Henry Wood and the author of *Molly Bawn*. I thought them quite beautiful of course, and the heroines most attractive, and it was some time before I got away from the terrible taste which such literature inevitably produces. I also read Miss Broughton who was a good deal better and who wrote one novel, *Cometh up as a Flower*, of which later in life I heard that charming man of letters, Monsieur Jusserand, say that it was the only novel he had ever read in English which had real passion. This was some time ago before Passion had become fashionable.

I now come to a childish incident which seems scarcely worth recording except that it had a great effect on my mentality. As I said above, I was always at war with Bachelor the nurse and she and I disliked each other cordially. One day my mother was away and the two Mackenzie girls and I were given the younger children to look after, I suppose because Bachelor wanted to do something else. My small sister Dot got very tired and I took her on my back. She was heavy for me and I slipped and fell, hurting the child, who cried very much. I was very frightened and asked her not to say anything about it. She seemed quite happy and ran about again in a short time and I thought no more of it. Next day there happened to be a children's party to which we all went, and in the middle of it Dot fell again and this time shrieked violently and said that she had had a pain all night and that Tiny had told her not to tell any one. There was a doctor there and he examined her and said the collar-bone was broken. Bachelor and the governess immediately turned on me and said that I had threatened my poor little sister not to tell about the bone. I need hardly say that I had no idea she was injured, but of course it was wrong of me not to tell of the accident at once. The only two people who believed that I had no idea how serious it was, were Mrs. Awdry, the wife of the Private Secretary, and Captain Gordon. They were very kind and did all they could to comfort me, but every one else was perfectly horrible and when my mother came back she really spoke as if I had tried to murder the child. I was dreadfully miserable and above all it gave me the settled conviction that one was up against the world and had only oneself to shift for one, which is a very bad thing for a child to feel. I felt that if one lot of people were going to be so dreadfully unfair, everybody would be.

In a way it is a good thing to feel that you have only yourself to trust to, but in another it makes you very cynical and very bitter. It took a great many years and a great deal of kindness from outside people to remove the impression that if one made a false step one's entourage would be on one like wolves. Everybody said, 'Oh, she is a cruel child.' I was a very odious child, conceited, rude and unpleasant in every way, but I do not think I ever was cruel. I had far too vivid an imagination to wish any one to suffer bodily pain. I once remember thrashing my dog and the way it cringed and then licked my boots as dogs do. It loved me all the more afterwards, but I was ashamed of myself and never did it again. But I never respected dogs after that. Other animals have too much pride to make friends with people who ill-treat them, but dogs are masochists.

It was during the winter when I was twelve that I began to go out at night and I was fortunately never caught. I used to roam about for hours on end in the woods and later on I initiated Hampden into these expeditions. We used to take a dog each on a leash and used to chase the pariah dogs. It was enormously amusing and did nobody any harm. I cannot think how we were never caught.

I was terribly naughty and was always leading the poor Mackenzies, who were good quiet girls, into mischief. One evening my mother had a great ball and I had been guilty of some misdemeanour, so I was not allowed to go down for the first few dances, which I was generally permitted to do. I collected the Mackenzies and we wandered about whilst the dinner preceding the dance was taking place, on mischief bent. Unfortunately we found a large bowl of candied sugar and the brilliant idea came to me to dribble sugar on to the dancers as they left the ballroom, rather hot, from a gallery that ran across the hall. So we hid and with infinite precautions, dropped the sugar. At first all went well, the guests grew stickier and stickier and could not imagine what was happening. At last rather too much sugar fell on Captain Bagot's mess uniform and with a yell of rage he left his partner and dashing upstairs seized me, shook me and carried me to my bedroom biting furiously. I will draw a veil over the next day.

But we did worse things than that, and one afternoon established ourselves on a hill overhanging the principal road to Government House, and amused ourselves by rolling rocks down so that they jumped over the road. We only just missed the dog-cart containing the staff, and I suddenly thought that I might have killed them all, and I must say that on that occasion I was not enraged by my very severe punishment, but thought it fair. And when Mrs. Mackenzie turned on me and told me I had ruined her daughters I felt a good deal of remorse, though I was, as I said before, an odious child, always seeking for new sensations and a horrible mixture of would-be grown-upness and infantile perversity.

About this time I realized that I had very queer eyes and could frighten people by staring at them very hard. This gave me great pleasure and I did it to one or two of the Indian servants who firmly believed that I was possessed with the Devil. I used to focus my eyes on them and then walk slowly towards them and they would drop dustpan or broom or whatever they were carrying and fly in terror to the godowns. This was very bad for my character, but extraordinarily amusing, and I did not realize till much later how wrong it was to frighten people.

I used to scare poor Hampden who was afraid of the dark by saying 'Eyes—eyes' to him in the night nursery. It was loathsome of me, but I did not know of course how serious it might have been for him. Years after, he described his terror and I was ashamed and sad.

We did not see very much of the native gentlefolk. The only one I remember with any distinctness was Daoud Shah, who was a prisoner of the British Government and lived at Ootacamund. He was the finest-looking man I ever saw, six feet eight inches in his bare feet and broad in proportion.

He used to come out hunting on a huge horse like a cart-horse and rode fearlessly and well. He had a delightful smile. The Maharajah of Mysore, a beautiful polo player and a charming gentleman, used to come fairly often and now and then my mother took me to a zenana to see the inmates, accompanied by an interpreter. The ladies spent the most enormous amount of money on mechanical toys, dogs that wound up and would walk about the room, dolls that spoke, little trains and horrible little inventions which they played with for one day and then probably smashed like other children. They never seemed to have anything to do, but I suppose some of them did their husbands' cooking and a certain amount of needlework when visits were not being paid. One or two were very beautiful, but the older ones were fat and plain. They all seemed very good-tempered and sweet to each other and there was no impression that they were unhappy. If they ill-treated each other they managed to hide it very cleverly from outside people. I remember one girl telling my mother how terribly she pined for her garden. She was a Mohammedan and came from the North and had had a big garden and when she came to Madras there was none and she missed all the freedom and exercise.

We saw few people except at lunch. Most of my days, when not occupied with my father, were spent in riding about the great hills either alone, or with my brother Hampden. We were both experts, and could saddle and bridle our horses and were quite to be trusted not to overtire our animals or bring them in too hot.

We had quantities of pets and they played a great part in our lives. The Maharajah of Mysore gave us a baby elephant, who was, however, not a very attractive pet as he was too large not to be frightening and at the same time was rather bad-tempered. He did not live very long, poor animal. Then I had at various times a minah who talked beautifully; a Malabar squirrel, a fierce beast, though he was tame with me; a green parrot and several dogs. One of these, a Yorkshire terrier, was killed by the pariah dogs and my father put a stone up to his memory and after a short time we found offerings of flowers put on this stone. Arthur Bagot discovered from his bearer that a great many of the people thought it was His Excellency's god who had been for some curious reason incarnated in a dog and who had better be propitiated.

But the nicest pet of all was a Sambhur fawn, who was the sweetest-tempered and most attractive beast I have ever known. He used to follow me everywhere and I often curled up in his shed in the hay with my head on his shoulder. I shared his affections with a handsome young groom called Raju, and we were both very miserable when he died of cold.

Looking back I am extremely grateful to my father and mother for leaving me so much alone just then. Whether it was intentional or whether it was because they were busy I never knew, but they left Hampden and me entirely to our own resources and the result was that we had two happy years.

What queer things we did. I went to a native wedding in the syces' quarters and sat on the floor amongst the guests. I crawled into a Toda hut and saw the one wife of seven brothers cooking. That was at Marly Mund. Hampden and I would ride up Doda Bet alone, 8,500 feet, telling our grooms to meet us at the top. We would go and play in the Tigers' Cave away on the opposite side of the valley. There was always the chance of seeing a tiger there and that added zest to what was already thrilling. Sometimes we were taken out pig shooting and after smaller game, and sometimes we went pig sticking or rather watched other people do it from a safe hill.

James Tagg let me drive a high dog-cart and I was learning to be a good whip when my mother found out. She gave us a small governess-cart but that ended disastrously, as the nursery party promptly upset. They are always dangerous things, too low for the driver to control the pony.

One wonderful week I spent at Kartary by the great waterfall, and another lovely week at Neddiwattum. And once we camped on the Droog, with a marvellous view straight down to the plains, thousands of feet below. Everything was so exquisite, the perfect camp, perfect servants, the scarlet rhododendrons flaming on every hill, the long rides through the sholas, and the marvellous moonlight nights. To be a child in India was a joy such as nothing in after life could ever be, and could I have those three years back I would willingly forget all the rest of my life.

The November before I was thirteen my mother decided to take me to the plains with them and leave Dot at Ootacamund. So I left the great hills and the wide free life. There were many pleasures at Guindy and Madras, but they were more grown-up pleasures, and my mother began to teach me. She was a first-rate teacher, but she taught dull subjects like *A Commentary on the Prayer Book* and History from heavy books. I learnt French and German poetry for her and, what was very valuable, wrote reviews of any book I read and accounts of the country round or any expeditions. I rode a good deal but did not enjoy it, my nerve went again the moment I got to the plains. My amusements were mostly solitary: to roam about the divine gardens or to pick flowers and fruit in the park, or to go to the sea accompanied by my guinea pig and hunt for shells. I was sometimes allowed to go to grown-up parties and Captain Bagot taught me to waltz. By thirteen I was a beautiful dancer and I wanted dreadfully to be a professional. It was my only real talent. I had facility for verse writing and music and a pretty voice, but my hands were bad and my throat weakened by too much reading aloud. But dancing I was really gifted for, and I wish my people had let me be trained either for that or to become a journalist.

I remember the first Lady Cromer, then Mrs. Baring, and Mr. Wilfrid Blunt and Lady Anne coming to stay. She was very kind to me, and so was Lady Ripon, who came with the Viceroy and their complete staff *en route* for Hyderabad, where we all went for the Installation of the Nizam. Lord Bill Beresford, most amusing of human beings, and Captain Charlie Burn, the handsomest man in the British Army, were in their train. It was like an Arabian Nights fairy-tale. The Installation was splendid beyond words, and the review magnificent, with the great salute of the elephants. And one day we went for a marvellous ride on elephants through the old town seeing all the wonder of costume, and looking in at windows no European had ever seen into before. The great elephant kraals impressed me very much, with elephants lying about on straw just as horses might in England.

I was frightened of elephants and agreed with the man who, describing an elephant ride, said, 'When you go up you feel you are going to the devil—but when you come down you feel that you are going to nothing at all.'

But the most marvellous experience of all was the great Banquet given by the Nizam to celebrate his installation. There were two hundred people and all were served on a service of gold plate, succeeded by marvellous china. I was given in charge to the Viceroy's secretary Mr., afterwards Sir, Henry Primrose, who was very kind. Later there was the finest display of fireworks and the whole Palace and the town were illuminated. It spoilt me for all succeeding parties as I always compared them and nothing has ever come up to it again in splendour or good taste. The Nizam was always one of the greatest friends of the English and a loyal ally, governing his kingdom wisely and well, and his son is following in his footsteps.

After this I went back to Ootacamund and spent a quiet month before my mother and Captain Bagot came up. I was delighted to get back to my mountains again and ran wild as before. By this time I had a Eurasian maid, Margaret, who was very unsatisfactory and taught me a lot of unnecessary knowledge about what is known as the 'facts of life', facts children are better without. I did not improve under her tuition and my mother awoke to the conviction that I was, as one might put it, 'in a bad way'. Prompted by Arthur Bagot, who saw I needed education and above all discipline, she settled in a few weeks for me to go to school at home, accompanying me herself to settle me.

One evening she broke the news. The shock was so awful that for some moments I could not speak at all, I nearly fainted. Then I went out of the room, locked myself in my bedroom and refused to let any one in. I think I was mad that night, but it ended in a sobbing fit that lasted about three hours. In the morning I was ill, but struggled up and came down, but was sent back to bed.

Of the misery of those months before I left India it is useless to write. It was a time of such concentrated agony that nothing later in the way of mental pain, and I have had plenty, ever touched my strength.

PET ELEPHANT

I thought of killing myself, but was afraid; I thought of getting some one to marry me, but knew that though I could have pulled it off had I been Miss Smith, as the Governor's daughter the act would have involved the man in too much scandal. I consulted with Margaret as to whether I could be smuggled away into some native prince's house. But she saw it was too difficult. So I gave in and with the apathy of despair began to prepare for the awful day, fixed for the 25th of April. Arthur Bagot understood and was endlessly kind, though he thought it the right thing for me. Mrs. Awdry also understood, and my father, who hated my going, understood a little though he could not say much. My mother could never comprehend why I should object to leaving India and was herself wild with joy at getting home.

Every detail of the last day is printed on my memory. Early that fated morning I went to my father and read as usual. By chance I began the poem,

'Say not the struggle naught availeth
The labour and the wounds are vain——'

of Arthur Clough's, finishing up with the line,

'But westward, look, the land is bright.'

'We will stop there,' said my father, his voice quivering a little. I could not cry. I was dumb with grief. The drive down, terribly frightening as it was, left me cold. I longed to be killed. When we got to Madras the great heat upset me and I was ill when we got on board ship.

Arthur Bagot held me tight in his arms. 'Poor little woman—dear little woman,' he whispered. 'It will not be so bad as it seems.' But it was much, much worse.

The voyage home—how different from the radiant voyage out! I did lessons with my mother, reading Turgenieff's *Mémoires d'un Seigneur Russe*, in the intervals of playing games about the ship with other passengers 'and flirting my little 'ead off', as Bachelor phrased it, with the officers.

But I had 'La mort au coeur' and no one but Mrs. Awdry, who was with us, understood. I owe her a deep debt of gratitude for her sympathy. Then the weather became cold and rough and I was miserably seasick, and worst of all I was not allowed to write to any one in India except my father.

The only incident of the return journey that I remember with any pleasure was my interest in a small child, Kitty Keyes, the daughter of the Admiral of that name, who at three was coming back from India with her mother. She was a lovely creature and for the first time I remember feeling what a pleasure it must be to have children, and how much I should like to have a child like Kitty. I had never had any maternal feeling for my own little sister Dot, who was a perfect child and very lovely but not in the least interesting. In later life she became an enchanting person and from fifteen on I cared for her more than I have ever cared for any woman, but she was curiously without interest as a child. Iseult, the sister born in India, was always ill and was quite a baby, so I had no interest in her either, and our nursery was so badly managed that the babies were unattractive objects and constantly screamed, which of course a healthy and well-kept baby ought not to do. Kitty was just at the most interesting age and I adored her. Later when I went to my cousin Lily Ainsworth's I found my own small sister Lily the same age, also a very beautiful and most engaging child.

Some girls have the maternal instincts

very early. There is an exquisite poem of Sir Arthur Quiller-Couch's which deals with a child of three. With many women, especially English women, it only awakens with the advent of a child, and many more literally never have it till they have grandchildren. It would be interesting to find out by psychoanalysis the factors that go to increasing or decreasing the maternal instincts. I have found with boys and girls brought up with many brothers and sisters that they have an instinctive horror of children and do not wish to have large families themselves and, equally, only children have an exaggerated idea of the pleasures of companionship. This is very natural, but there are probably much more obscure causes for the fact that some women desire children at an early age and others have no wish for them. It is rare to find a man who does not want to have children, but this is doubtless because they have none of the trouble of them and look upon them as amusing playthings to be seen on Sundays when there is nothing better to do.

We stopped at Marseilles and I was amused by the quays and the queer beasts and birds and shells for sale there, but

A VICTORIAN CHILDHOOD

always at the back of my mind was the exile's longing for home.

And so one cold afternoon in May we arrived at Tilbury and went to lodgings in Oxford Terrace, where my brothers had taken rooms. I can never pass through the Westbourne Place district without recalling my horror of England. The dull dismal streets, the, to me, hideous people, in drab clothes, the ugliness of it all. And I was so cold.

My brothers seemed the same. They no longer persecuted me physically, but they showed me unmistakably that they thought me dreadful, which I undoubtedly was. Conceited, lazy, self-indulgent and with a tongue that could defend its proprietor. I was that unpleasant creature, a flapper who longed to be treated like a grown-up person. That I was immensely interested in all life did not interest them, who were only interested in the life of those who possessed the attributes known as good form.

CHAPTER VI

NOTHING happened during those grey days in London of any moment except that I went to my first opera, *Aïda*, and was horribly disappointed. I suppose I had a developed dramatic sense even then, for the absurdity of the Italian opera struck me very forcibly. Instead of being thrilled I merely thought it comic, and the music, after Schumann and Schubert and Beethoven, to which I was accustomed, seemed very obvious. I was not sufficiently musical to know what a great master of his own craft Verdi is, and merely judged it from the artistic impression of the whole.

At the end of a month we went down to Northampton to stay with my mother's cousin, Dick Ainsworth, at his hunting box, Winwick Warren. Northamptonshire is a dull county, with the worst faults of an English landscape, but its dullness is made exquisite at the end of May by the great masses of hawthorn on every hedge. I was thankful to get out of London, and when Dick's wife held out her arms saying, 'So this is Tiny'—I felt for the first time pleasure in England. She was one of those women whom it is very difficult to describe. She was quite ugly, with a receding forehead, protruding eyes and a weak chin, and had no claim to beauty except beautiful teeth and a good complexion and very white hands. But I do not think I ever met anybody, man, woman or child, who did not fall in love with her straight off and remain her devoted slave all their life. She was not particularly clever, except as a psychologist, and though she had never read a book on the subject, and knew nothing of the conclusions which experts have come to, she had by sheer sympathy found out most of the data that it takes years of hard study for the average human being to arrive at. She had immense humour, but of a kind so delicate that most people never suspected her of it, and an innate refinement which was perhaps commoner in those days than it is now. She instinctively shrank from everything ugly or vulgar or unworthy, and yet nobody tackled pain and wretchedness, and even sin more bravely than she did, whenever it was her duty to approach it. She was the most deeply religious woman I ever knew and I wish that the form it took had not been that of old-fashioned Evangelicalism, which led her into strange paths and company. It was only with regard to religious persons that her marvellous judgment of character was ever at fault. If a person professed to be a sincere Christian, it was very difficult for Nono to believe that he was a hypocrite, and many undeserving people took advantage of this and gained great ascendancy over her.

But I was far too young to realize all this during my first stay at Winwick. I merely saw her as gay and tender and infinitely understanding, the first person who was the least sorry for me at having to leave India and all my friends. She mothered and petted me and gained my full confidence, so that my one idea when we left was to get back to her. Her husband was a good solid Lancashire squire, Tory to the backbone, a good rider, and a good shot, a perfect example of the English gentleman of the old school. He considered that Poacher and Radical were almost identical terms, and that both meant blackguards of the worst kind.

We went back to London after a fortnight and then the dismal day arrived when my mother was to take me to Cheltenham and leave me there for five weeks. After the summer holidays I was to return for good.

It was a hot June day and Cheltenham was at its loveliest. Few of the Anglo-Indian colonels and the retired dowagers who go there for sport and cards realize what a romantic town it is, with its spacious Regency Houses and its wealth of flowering trees and shrubs. But the beauty of the place struck the small rebellious child who was being taken from India to go to school under Miss Beale, the then very modern head of the Ladies' College, and one of the few great educators in this country or indeed anywhere.

My culminating horror was that I was going to school. Like all rather clever children I had a horror of the herd, the herd mentality, herd games, herd morals and manners, and I had not yet realized that even in the herd if you show it that you are not afraid of it, you can practically do what you like.

My mother and I arrived at the Queen's Hotel one morning and after the usual English lunch, proceeded to interview my new house mistress, to whom I took an instant and violent dislike. We then proceeded to the Ladies' College, a frightful building, perhaps the ugliest in England, which did not tend to mend matters in my mind. But when we went into the little house alongside the College, and the grave, rather beautiful woman rose to receive us, I realized that in Miss Beale there was something a little different, something not common, something apart. She was short, but her dignity was marvellous. The only person of her generation whose dignity was greater was Queen Victoria. She had large penetrating eyes and great humour in the corners of her mouth. She walked with an extraordinarily smooth long step, it must have been because she wore no heels. It was a sight to see her come up the long hall and fall upon some luckless child who had caught her attention from the further end.

She shook hands with my mother and myself and then sat down and had the usual conversation which parents have with the heads of institutions. But all the time she was talking to my mother, she was really watching me and taking in my immense indignation. When we left she shook hands in a friendly way saying, 'You must come and see me the first day you are at College, I shall send for you.' And the interview was over.

Next morning my mother left me at Lansdowne Villa, Miss Eales' house. Two of the elder girls, Gladys Sandwith and Dinah Flower, were for some reason not at College that day and they very kindly and condescendingly came to help me unpack. I, used to giving orders, and knowing exactly what I wanted done, thanked them and proceeded to tell them where to stow my belongings, with the help of a hammer and nails I had brought with me. Their astonishment knew no bounds and they were so *verblüfft*, that they meekly did as I commanded. When I said, 'No, two inches lower' or 'You've got it too much to the left', they obediently hearkened. But they registered black marks against this appallingly conceited and cocksure child and I never heard the last of that morning. 'The damnedest cheek we ever met,' was their verdict.

A VICTORIAN CHILDHOOD

It was the day of the school exeat and after lunch we proceeded to Weston-super-Mare where the house was to stay over Sunday. These half-term breaks were very pleasant in my schooldays and I am sorry they are given up. A girl seized on me that afternoon and told me Miss Eales wished us to be friends. I was quite prepared, and for twenty-four hours we were inseparable. She taught me many strange things in those twenty-four hours. At the end of that time we quarrelled violently and scarcely ever spoke to each other again. But I had learned a lot.

After this every one tried to bully me. Of physical bullying there was none, thank God. That is the only thing that breaks a child. No one can stand up against physical pain. But everything that sneers, innuendoes, accusations of snobbism, of conceit, of want of manners, that could be applied, was applied. I minded, but it never touched me on the raw, for none of these people seemed to me to matter. Coming as I did from a very cultivated home I saw they were ignorant and was too green to realize that there were plenty of interesting and valuable girls amongst them. That was to come later. And I saw that I knew technically twice as much as the other girls of my own age. That meant that I took an excellent place in College and that I could do with really very little effort the work required of me. I had also a very sharp tongue and a ready wit, and though that term I was hideously unpopular I managed to hold my own. Miss Beale sent for me very soon and was intensely kind. And she put me into the class of Miss Laurie, whom I liked, and who, having taught all my daughters, still remains a valued and honoured friend. I was very grateful to her for helping an ignoramus to find her feet.

When the holidays came, we went first to Smithills Hall, my cousin Richard Ainsworth's real home. Next to Guindy I think it is the house that has been most to me of all those that I have lived in. It is a splendid old black-and-white timbered hall, standing in a great park close to the town of Bolton-le-Moors. The oldest part is King John, but the building is very much older than that and it is said that a house of that name stood there as far back as 597, though this of course is merely legend. It was here that the Martyr, Richard Marsh, was tortured under Queen Mary, and as they led him from being racked, he put his poor bleeding foot down on the stone pavement and said, 'As sure as my Faith is the right one, this mark will remain.' The mark is certainly still there and it does not do to tamper with it. Some foolish young men removed the stone and threw it into the shrubbery some fifty years before I first went there. The most disastrous manifestations followed and every one was so terrified by noises and the feeling of being touched by invisible things, that they very soon put it back and everything became quiet.

One room was always kept, in the rather grisly way of our fathers, as the place in which any deceased member of the family was laid out. This room was called the 'Dead Room' until Lily Vaughan married my cousin, Richard Ainsworth. She said it was barbarous and would not have it so named. It had always been used as a spare bedroom in spite of this unpleasing title, but none of us very willingly slept there, and I myself thought the whole wing of the house haunted. There was supposed to be the ghost of a cat in this wing and one day after a group of very rowdy cousins had

DOROTHEA BEALE

been chaffing about the animal, three of us came down to breakfast next morning with long scratches on our faces which nobody could account for. We spoke with great caution on the subject after this.

The moors came down to the edge of the park and were as beautiful as Scottish ones in spite of the great manufacturing town so close, and there were acres of lovely garden and the town was cleverly planted out with trees so that the place never felt the least suburban. My granduncle's old home, Moss Bank, which marched with it, held all the near property, so it was a perfect home for children as the country-side belonged to us and we were always treated as the children of the house, my cousins having none of their own.

The bleaching works too, which were a family property in which every man, woman and child had grown up serving Ainsworths, was a great joy to us, and we were always wandering round watching the processes, inhaling the pungent odours of the bleaching works, which we honestly liked. A strange taste! The mill hands were almost like part of the family. Old men would say, 'Ah, you are the daughter of Julia who was the daughter of Hannah who was the daughter of old Mr. Ainsworth up t' Hall.' They never remembered anybody's name when they married, but they always remembered them by their Christian names. The servants of the estate and many of the mill hands came to Smithills Chapel twice on Sunday. When we arrived a new Chaplain was just installed, a Mr. Standen, who was to revolutionize the old house, which was run on the lines of every big country house in those days, very lavishly. Mr. Standen was a man of great force with an uncanny knack of getting at people's souls. This power he used to both spiritual and other advantages. We all hated him, but admitted his power. He tried very hard to convert us all in groups and singly, I must say without much success. At one time he got me as far as the Penitents' bench when I was fifteen, a most inflammable age, and I remember walking in a Salvationist procession with a trumpet, but the emotion did not last. He took an enormous hold on my cousin and his wife and for many years practically ruled Smithills. He got rid of the old servants and filled the house with missionaries, some good and some bad. But the whole character of the place was very much changed and it was no longer what it had been, a charming meeting-ground for numbers of people. This did not mercifully prevent an excellent cook being kept and a great standard of comfort being adhered to. Nono always said firmly that she did not believe Almighty God the least wished us to be uncomfortable, and I always think that that was a very sound view of the situation. But she expected us to attend countless prayer meetings and endless talks on religious subjects, and if she had not been so charming I suppose we should have jibbed, but we were all so fond of her that we accepted the drawbacks of the place without question, merely grumbling about Mr. Standen to each other, and I am ashamed to say, setting booby-traps for him. He must have dreaded the holidays, poor man.

It was at Smithills that I read an account in the *War Cry* of the White Slave Traffic. I shall never forget my horror and misery. I wrote an impassioned poem on the subject and asked Mr. Standen to get it published for me. He was rather impressed, but Nono was terribly shocked at my knowing about such things and promptly burnt it. From this moment I was a convinced feminist.

That first summer at home my mother and I went to the Isle of Man to stay with the Governor, Sir Spencer Walpole, and afterwards to stay with Sir James Stephen, the great judge. Sir Spencer and Lady Walpole were like a second mother and father to me and treated me exactly as if I had been a sister of their own daughter Maud. I went there every summer holidays and both Sir Spencer and his wife had a great effect on my character. She was very beautiful, had a remarkably clear and fastidious mind, and a cold, pure, critical taste in literature and art.

The summer holidays in the Isle of Man were a delight. It was too icy to bathe, I tried it once or twice, but those Northern seas are not agreeable. The walks were exquisite, over the great hills covered with purple heather and down to enchanting little bays like Maughold with longer expeditions to Peel Castle and the Bishop's Palace. In the mornings I sat up in an old apple-tree or an equally old laburnum, reading through Keats, Shelley, Byron, Lamartine, Carlyle, —I always liked my literature in chunks.

A VICTORIAN CHILDHOOD

In the afternoon Sir Spencer played tennis with Maud and me or we went for long walks. In the evenings Lady Walpole read to us or we talked and knitted. I remember the awe with which I saw Sir Spencer read a volume of Grotes' history per week, quite absorbed and oblivious of the chatter around him. On another occasion he was found sobbing in the library over the account of Waterloo in Mrs. Ewing's *Jackanapes*. He put the paragraph beginning, 'There are killed and wounded by the war of whom no returns reach Downing Street', very high and said he defied any one to read it out loud without their voice shaking. Spencer Walpole was one of the very best men I ever came across and the most typical Englishman. Not imaginative, in some ways slow, he had an amazingly far seeing, logical, sensible mind and great practical ability. One of the turning-points in my moral life was when, having been caught smoking, Sir Spencer took me out for a long walk and put the fear of God into me. He was very downright, even brutal, and he woke me up to the fact that small deceits practised habitually led to larger deceits later on. I sobbed my heart out in bed that night and my lovely white lady as I used to call her, for she had snow-white hair and an exquisite young face, came up when she saw I was really sorry and forgave me. If only the middle aged of the present day realized how much harm they do by condoning the wrongdoings of children they would hesitate about their sloppy 'Oh, they will grow up all right' attitude.

A number of people used to come to stay during those summer holidays. I remember the geologist, Mr. Boyd Dawkins and Marta Barnewitz, a beautiful musician, a pupil of Henselt, and the Bishop of Sodor and Man, Dr. Hill, a jovial cleric not much given to talk shop. There was a tragic episode once, when Maud's dear old ex-governess, an ancient and very pious German lady called Madé, had been looking forward for weeks to seeing the Bishop, and after the great party to receive him was over, and she was asked if all had come up to her expectations, she said rather sadly that she had loved the band and the tent and the red cloth and being treated like royalty. But she added, 'The Bishop said no word of the Lord Jesus.'

The Isle of Man was rather overcrowded with trippers, but it was not the sort of enormous tea garden it is now, and was very like Galloway, a sort of miniature Highlands with a much better climate. It was an enchanting place and I first learnt to love the Northern sea there. The coast was very like Aberdeenshire, and I suppose it is partly due to my being there as a child and partly atavism that I have such a passion for the North.

It is certain that all our sympathies were always Scottish. And I remember from my very earliest years being glad that I was a Scot and frankly despising all who were not. I am sure it was nothing that my father ever said, for his dictum on the subject was that the best way to behave was to live in England and rave about Scotland, and my mother hated Scotland. My two elder brothers had been brought up there and were sorry to leave it, but none of us younger ones ever lived there as children. But the fact remains that Scotland was our Mecca and my poor mother used to say that none of her children had ever forgiven her for being English. Even now, when I get to Banff and the funny little train stops at the toy station like something off a Christmas tree and I see the waves tumbling against the bar of sand,

A VICTORIAN CHILDHOOD

and the Duff woods stretching up the valley, it is as much as I can do to prevent the tears coming to my eyes. Scottish folk are like that, so are the Irish. The English have so many colonies and are so linked up with Empire that little England and its sights and sounds and smells does not mean the same to them as it does to people whose country is poor and small. They want to be British, not English. We want to be Scots, not Britons.

My mother and I went on from the Isle of Man to the Mourne Mountains which were equally lovely. Sir James Stephen had a house there for many years called Anaverna. They were good people, but curiously *rêche* and unresponsive, and I was always rather alarmed by the whole family, with the exception of Herbert. Jim Stephen, the famous J. K. S., was very handsome in a heavy way, and extremely witty also in a heavy way. The Maybrick case was going on at the time and was very much on Sir James's mind. They also read *Treasure Island* out loud and I was thrilled. I always thought Sir James Stephen must have been like Judge Jeffreys, but as a matter of fact he was extremely kind and just and it was a most unfair impression, but children get these ideas into their heads and nothing will get them out. The nicest of the family was Catherine who was for many years head of Newnham College, and I was very fond of Herbert too.

We then went to stay with Lord Coleridge at Ottery St. Mary, in Devon, and I was immensely struck by Mr. Stephen Coleridge with his exquisite ascetic face.

At the end of the holidays we were at York House. My brothers were always trying to get hold of my precious diary, in which I recorded not only facts, but all my beliefs and feelings, as is the way of young things. I left it one day when I was out in charge of Bachelor, who promised not to read it or let it out of her hands. She gave it to Evelyn and my brothers read the cherished volume and told my mother of its contents. Bachelor's excuse was that my brothers went to her and said that I told them to ask her for it, but of course it was a put-up job. My mother sent for me and spoke to me very seriously about the 'dreadful revelations' of character shown by the diary. She did not however seem the least shocked at either the treachery of

Bachelor or of my brothers. She said she had not read it but would if I preferred her to. I said no, the whole thing was soiled and desecrated and I would like it burnt. She was terribly hurt but burnt it before my eyes. That finished any hope of affection between any of us and in a way it was a good thing. I no longer disliked my brothers, I simply never thought of them at all. Before, I had a lurking suspicion that they might be my superiors and were right in despising me, but this treachery about the diary put them immeasurably below me morally and I never considered their opinions for a moment again.

Later on in life Arthur and I became great friends and have continued very intimate ever since. He married a most attractive American, Kathleen Clayton, daughter of General Clayton who was American Ambassador in Mexico. He would never have persecuted me of himself, but he was afraid of the others.

CHAPTER VII

IN September my mother took me back to Cheltenham and left me at Lansdowne Villa. This going back was not nearly so dreadful, as it was not straight from India and I felt I knew the worst. I had been put into a new class, the first class of the second division under Miss Knott. Miss Knott was an excellent teacher, always beautifully dressed in a silk gown rather tightly made which swished about on the polished floors. She was quite unlike her second-in-command, a brisk young woman, Miss Mold, a product of the modern school. I was very fond of both of them and liked my class. The German and French teachers, Mademoiselle Kramer and Fräulein Schmidt, were also first-rate but bad-tempered and terrifying. However, they all made us work, which is the most important point, and were very just, and after my first year I went up into the first division and did French and German under Mademoiselle Ruchet and

Fräulein von Borries, two delightful and gifted women who were as kind as they could be and brilliant teachers. The discipline was excellent and I was happy in College. I was happy in my house too, but I do not think it was a very wholesome happiness. The conversation of certain pupils was like any barrack-room, and they naturally tried to get hold of new girls as recruits. However, there were plenty of clean nice-minded girls as well, and one was very soon able to distinguish between them.

I disliked my house mistress very much at first, then came absolutely under her influence and adored her, then finally returned to my first impression. She was a clever woman and I owe her a deep debt of gratitude for making me hear Wagner before most people in England knew anything about him. She was a great friend of Malten, the famous *prima donna*. She described Bayreuth and its marvels to me and would have taken me there had my parents let me go.

Looking at Cheltenham to-day and thinking of what it was then, I should think that it was in some ways a safer place for girls to go to, as the supervision is so strict that it is almost impossible for a girl to learn any evil, on the other hand she learns very much less good than she did during my time there.

The intimacy of other young things was most useful in developing the mind and character and there was none of that attempt at creating a type which is such a tragic thing in all big schools nowadays. We played tennis, but we were not *made* to play tennis, we could go for walks over the lovely country if we liked. We did a certain amount of what were called calisthenics but they were not very exhausting, unless a girl had need of special exercises. There was plenty of dancing and the music was very much better than it is now, and the intellectual interests of girls much more acute. I suppose this was partly because a woman of genius was at the head of things and because she had the wisdom to choose very remarkable women as her assistants and to leave them a great deal of liberty. The class mistresses knew their girls well, had them to tea two or three times a term and were interested in their pursuits and their point of view. It was not a question of size, for Cheltenham in my time reached nearly eight hundred girls, but it was the difference in the attitude to life of those in charge.

Miss Beale did not particularly care whether people passed examinations or not, though she was glad of course when they did. What she wanted was to make fine women who would influence their generation. Her own deep religious feelings had an immense effect on the school, and I shall never forget the impression I received as a quite young girl when I heard her read the first chapter of St. John's Gospel. It was quite electric, one felt that this woman was reading the thing she considered the greatest in the world and that she was somehow putting over to a class of little geese, that it was immensely important. Afterwards I often heard her expound it, and I always wish that she had left in writing some definite memoranda of her teaching on the subject. I fancy many of her old pupils would admit that she made the Last Gospel the most vital thing in their lives.

There were a lot of clever girls in my house. The ones I remember best were Lily Scowcroft, Amy Turner, Hildegarde Muspratt, Josephine Evans Williams, and Blanche Coventry, who were great friends by turns. Anybody who has been to school knows, one term one might be at daggers drawn and the next intimate friends, but these girls I remember with real affection. In those days we were not allowed to see very much of girls outside our houses, but my greatest friend at College was one in another house, Mabel Cartwright, an interesting creature and a fine musician, and what the Germans call a 'Charaktermensch'. She is now the head of a big school in Toronto. I owe a great deal to my admiration of her, for I was always trying to live up to her standard even though I failed dismally.

The second year I was at College I was put into the Oxford class, in the first division, under Miss Buckle and Miss Aitken. They were both able teachers and I was devoted to them. I managed to pass the Senior Oxford at fifteen and a half and then moved up into Miss Soulsby's class. She had only just come to Cheltenham and was one of the most remarkable women of her day and one of the only four great educationalists I have met in my life. Miss Beale was one, she was another, Gabrielle Rossignon was the third and Mrs. Boole was the fourth. I suppose it is the rarest of human gifts and probably the most important. She would see the possibilities in a block of a child coming from any kind of nondescript home and would train it in a year or two into a human being worth having. I can still recall our first class with her. We trooped into No. 2A silently as usual and settled down knowing that a new teacher was coming, and then suddenly from the other side of the platform, rose the ugliest woman I have ever seen. She must have been six feet two inches and every single thing about her was ugly, ungainly and badly made. With a huge mouth and shapeless nose, there was nothing to recommend her, but most of her class learnt to worship that ugly face before she had been with us for a year. She could make us cry and she could make us laugh. I remember the whole form being in tears over the execution of Charles I and over Rossetti's 'King's Tragedy'. She drummed English literature into us willy-nilly. And even the least sensitive were trained into some kind of interest in poetry when they were allowed to choose the pieces they were to learn. I was in Miss Soulsby's class when she gave her famous lectures on the last chapter of Proverbs, 'The Virtuous Woman'. I was inclined, as all schoolgirls and especially pretty schoolgirls were, to think that nothing except social, with perhaps a few intellectual attainments thrown in, were of any particular value. Miss Soulsby rammed into my head, once for all, that every woman should know about housekeeping, the direction of a household, needlework, cooking, catering and enough of public affairs to be able to discuss them with her menfolk ('Her husband shall be known in the Gates'). And all from the last chapter of Proverbs! She imbued us with a real love of the Bible, as did Miss Beale. We were never worried with the Journeys of St. Paul or long dissertations on what this or that complicated phrase meant. And no one ever made us learn the Revised Version. To my horror, when one of my daughters was at Cheltenham I heard that the unfortunate children were taught out of the Revised Version. Mr. Yeats, the poet, was going down to lecture one day soon after, and I begged him to speak on the subject, which he did. He was as horrified as I was, condemning it in no measured terms. I suppose the Revised Version has done more mischief to religion in England than any other factor. It has made the Bible a definitely boring Book and few young people read it nowadays. I do not wonder, I also should never have been *Bibelfest* had I been brought up on the Revised Version. The evil of the modern phraseology is especially noticeable amongst the country poor. The older people use the magnificent phrases of the Authorized Version and their speech has a weight and dignity which is completely lacking in the young.

Miss Soulsby was very human. She read our own poetry and criticized it, even my impassioned love lyrics she did not laugh at too much but tried to show me how to prune them, and we carried all our private troubles to her as well.

Another interesting teacher was Miss Margaret Robertson who, as far as I can remember, instructed me in logic. She was followed by Miss Amy Hutchisson Sterling, a daughter of the Scottish philosopher. I recall one holidays going to see him at Edinburgh and spending a delightful evening with him.

My mathematics were deplorable and I never could learn the simplest thing about drawing maps or the use of compasses. The only mistress I found impossible to get on with was a Miss ——, an admirable teacher but lacking in humour. I remember trying to explain to her that my mathematical diagrams were more valuable than those of the other pupils as mine were all hand drawn. I also remember an awful occasion when, during a lecture about geology and the strata in which trilobites occur, I had written out with appropriate illustrations the beautiful poem of May Probyn:

>　'How wonderful it seemed, how right
>　　　The providential plan,
>　That he should be a trilobite,
>　　　And I should be a man.'

She was very angry and I had to go back to College after lunch. 'Returns', as they were called, were a great disgrace, and one dreaded very much going back to College in the afternoon.

Christmas was spent at Smithills.

I do not know whether any book has ever been written about the connexion of scents with memory, but certain houses have curiously defined scents which seem to bring back in a moment everything connected with them. When I smell Windsor soap, I see the long passages at Smithills, the roaring fires against the black panelling, the texts hung promiscuously about, the faint odour of evergreens—Christmas decorations stayed up there longer than anywhere else—an occasional whiff of potpourri, Nono seated in an arm-chair by the fire, a boy or girl on the ground leaning against her knees, Cousin Dick reading the *Times* and interjecting angry comments on the heinousness of the Radicals. Prayers were at nine and the day never passed without some child being taken for 'a little word' with Nono or Cousin Dick about religious matters. Off some of us it rolled as water off a duck's back. But I remember trying desperately hard to be 'saved' and never quite understanding what it meant. 'Give your heart to Jesus,' said Nono, but at fifteen one is not certain what one's heart is, and a boy's, and much more, 'a girl's will is as the winds will. And the thoughts of youth are long long thoughts.'

At moments the religious bias was distressingly comic. Nono, for instance, who was a mystic in very truth, would entirely forget that she was at lunch, surrounded by a greedy group of boys and girls and, lost in ecstasy, would murmur, her eyes closed and her head thrown back, 'Jesus—Jesus, my Redeemer. To think that I shall see Him, shall touch His Hands.' And then suddenly waking to the realities of life she would exclaim, '*Dick*, if you eat more of that pudding, you *know* you will have an attack of gout.' But it never entered our heads to laugh any more than it enters the heads of an Indian village to laugh at the vagaries of its Holy man. Children know sanctity when they see it.

Once whilst I was there a mill girl, just converted, insisted upon being baptized by immersion. There were no conveniences for such a rite, so after endless discussion a large bath was introduced into the chapel and the radiant catechumen, wrapped in mackintoshes, was forcibly pressed under the water by Mr. Standen, after which joyful hymns burst from the congregation. I begged to be allowed to assist, but Nono said, 'No, darling, I *know* you would laugh.' I felt certain I should, so I had to stay outside.

We treated the various divines and missionaries who came to stay very differently.

I remember one morning when I was the only one at Smithills and a mission was going on. Five clergymen were at the breakfast table, and towards the close I, who had come in late, heard my neighbour suddenly say to my intense horror, 'There is one amongst us who is not saved. Now is the appointed time. Our Lord says, "When two or three are gathered together ———" Let us all pray that she also may find Salvation.' My cousins and the five clergymen fell on their knees and prayed with the greatest fervour for me, while I sat eating marmalade to cover my confusion, and feeling unutterably foolish. At the end they rose and sat with their eyes closed, expecting a miracle. But no miracle happened. I said, 'Thank you very much', and went on with my marmalade. But these people are right. If a man really believes in this curious conception of the Creator, then he has no choice but to behave as they did.

On another occasion I was staying at Smithills with a young Salvationist, a handsome and attractive boy who took immense pains to convert me. I asked him one day, 'Why are you bothering so much about me, there are five other women in the house, they've all got souls?'—'Ah, but think,' he said, 'with your face what you could do for the Lord.' That seemed to me horribly immoral—the idea of using prettiness to convert people. But perhaps it was more logical than appears at first sight. Anyway, I have never had the faintest wish to join the evangelical school. I respect their earnestness, but they have no sense of beauty in worship and their personal conceit, fostered by a religion which has no definite rules and standards but those set by chance ministers, is curiously unpleasant unless found in a person like Lily Ainsworth, who would have been a saint even if she had been a voodoo worshipper, and whose charm was proof against any absurdity.

The little chapel used to be crowded every Sunday with the employees on the estate, the mill hands, in fact every one who was within walking distance. We used to sing Ancient and Modern Hymns, varied by Moody and Sankey, and Mr. Standen, who had been ordained as an English priest, used to follow the Church of England service up to a certain point. He was a clever preacher and had an immense influence on the mill girls who used to come up to the Penitents' bench at the Revivalist Meetings and pour forth the story of their past lives. As far as I can make out, the movement called Buchmanism, which is attracting so much of the youth of Oxford, is precisely on the same lines as Moody and Sankey, who were just then starring all over England.

My brothers, influenced by Mrs. Ainsworth, treated me quite well. They took me out snap-shooting with them and we spent comfortable holidays. I marvel, looking back, at the contentment of children with scarcely anything to amuse them in a quiet old country house in bitter weather. An occasional day's skating, an occasional ride, long walks and a few days' rabbit-shooting and practice with revolvers. Nothing to do in the evenings but play chess or backgammon, and heaps of books to read. And yet we were absolutely happy and only asked that the holidays might last for ever.

That winter I was fifteen we were absorbed by *Frank Fairleigh*, *Verdant Green*, *Guy Livingstone*, Charles Lever and Scott and a thrilling work called *The House on the Marsh*. I began to read 'serious' books, starting with Law's *Serious Call* and Jeremy Taylor.

It was a struggle. I had to say to myself that I would read so many pages and read them—the best way to start serious reading. It became easier every day and the habit of concentration is soon formed.

I forget if it was this holidays or at a later date that I first met Esmé Pigott at Smithills. She was a niece of Mrs. Ainsworth's and we have remained friends to this day.

When I went back to Cheltenham I fell under the spell of my music teacher, Miss Amy Hare, and for a year or so she was the person that mattered most in my life. A woman of genius, who has never had the recognition she deserved owing to delicate health, she is now the head of the music in Welwyn Garden City, and I am told a power for good there. She it was who found out at once what I had never realized, that I would never be able to play well because my hands were far too small and unless they grew enormously it was useless to expect to be a pianist and my voice, though sweet and true, was not big enough to be worth training. This was one of the great sorrows of my life; I have never understood how any one really gifted can ever bother about marriage or any other of the careers open to women.

There were many faults in the Cheltenham of my day. We wore whatever clothes we liked and there was a lot of foolish emulation and endless discussion about frocks. Also there was a great deal of very undesirable conversation and too much discussion of lovers and love. The adoption of a plain simple uniform is a marked improvement and the school gymnastics and exercises have done good.

A certain amount of compulsory games may also be an advantage, but in my humble opinion this is very much overdone, and the constant scurrying is bad for growing children. They never have a moment to themselves and the old delightful intimacies are not encouraged. Also the whole artistic and literary interest of the children seems to me to be less. I remember when some one brought back Swinburne's *Poems and Ballads* and half the house went mad over it and we copied most of the book because we could not afford to buy it. When Hildegarde Muspratt smuggled in *The Story of an African Farm*, just out, the whole sky seemed aflame and many of us became violent feminists. (I was one already.) We also fought fiercely over politics. But it seems to me better to go mad over Shelley and Swinburne and Olive Schreiner than over the detective stories and silly, though harmless novels which are the intellectual food of most girls to-day. And I would rather a girl of mine left her school a wild red Home Ruler and Feminist than that she left it unable to take anything seriously except athletics and cinemas. The devil in the schoolgirl is thrown out, perhaps, by organized games, strict discipline and such constant occupation that she finds no time to get into mischief. But to the swept and garnished vacuum what seven devils enter in, when she has left her carefully guarded scholastic establishment?

It was when I was in Miss Soulsby's class that Miss Beale made me read Plato in Jowett's translation and it affected me deeply. Here was crystallized the philosophy that had always been mine unconsciously and which now became a definite bias in my life. About this time I was confirmed, and came under the influence of a very remarkable man, Canon Childe, who was then the incumbent of Christchurch. He was not only a fine preacher but a very great help to his confirmees. And specially so as he allowed us to state our doubts and difficulties without either snubbing us or trying to evade them. I remember his beginning one lecture: 'One of you came to me and said, "Mr. Childe, I cannot be confirmed, I do not believe in the Athanasian Creed." And I said to her: "My dear child, if it is any comfort to you to know it, I don't either." '—He paused a full minute and then said, 'Not as you take it. But——' and then followed the most magnificent dissertation on the great creed that could be imagined, one which certainly made me accept it and not only accept it but glory in it. Years after I told the mathematician, Mrs. Boole, and she laughed and said, 'I could no more get along without the Athanasian Creed than I could go out walking without my backbone.' She herself wrote an interesting paraphrase of it which is far less known than it ought to be.

I often go back to Cheltenham now and wander about the beautiful old roads. The centre of the town has changed very little and remains, to my mind, the most attractive one I know in England. And other generations of young girls are passing

A VICTORIAN CHILDHOOD

swiftly in crocodiles along the streets, where, from behind thickets of lilac and laburnum, the faint tinkle of pianos still echo the old classics. Do they, as we did, lie awake in the summer gloaming, the scent of hawthorn filling their rooms, and long for life and love and wish that their schooldays were over? Or are they being gradually moulded into the tragic pattern of the British schoolboy, the ideal of head mistresses, the member of the herd, with the herd mentality, the herd consciousness, ashamed of everything but herd instincts. I have a shrewd suspicion that in spite of the pressure applied many remain the sentimental sensuous creatures of my day, but their gods are Ramon Navarro and Ivor Novello, and other cinema stars and their favourite books are the works of Ethel Mannin and Seamark.

CHAPTER VIII

THE Christmas I was sixteen my mother came back from India bringing my three sisters, Dot, Lily and Iseult, with her to York House. I was preparing for a piano exam. and was very pleased to find that she had put a piano in my bedroom for me to practise, but then to my horror I found she also expected me to do the house-keeping and teach my three small sisters, which made serious practising impossible.

This was the only time I can remember not getting on perfectly with my sisters. Every child hates lessons instinctively and the person who presides over them comes in for her share of dislike, but we were always great friends from the day I left school till the day I married, with the exception of that one holiday. That vacation was altogether not a success as I had to give up my examination through not being properly prepared. But in one way it was a

A VICTORIAN CHILDHOOD

memorable Christmas, for I realized how intense was Adrian's passion for Scotland. He of all of us cared most for the traditions of the family, and was the first person who told me anything about them. My cousin Rachel Grant Duff (she dropped Ainslie directly she came of age and called herself Grant Duff) was also very absorbed in the past of the race, and did much to memorize it.

My father's family came from Banffshire, he was a third cousin of the last Duke of Fife, a Duff of the red and not the black Duffs, with auburn hair, very keen blue eyes and an extraordinarily white skin. Only one of us was a red Duff and that was my sister Lily who married Gerald Collier, a son of the second Lord Monkswell. She was so typical that walking through a village in Galway, she heard a man say as she passed a cottage door, 'If that is not a Duff face I'll eat my hat.' She turned and went inside and said, 'Who knows the Duffs here?' And she found it was an old Scotsman who came from Banffshire, and they had a long talk. My own daughter, Anne Marie, is also a red Duff. When I first took her to Banff I was talking to the old tinsmith, Peter

Lyon, who knew my people, at the door of his shop and the child passed. 'It's varra easy to see where *she* comes from,' he said. My cousin Aloys was a black Duff.

My father's Duff ancestors, I am sorry to say, were on the wrong side during the rebellion of Fifteen, though the Grants followed their lawful lord and were mostly captured and sent to the Colonies as slaves. But John Duff of Bowmakellach (born in 1624 and son of Adam Duff of Clunybeg) was out with Montrose in 1645 and again in 1650 and was saved in a dramatic way. After the defeat at Carbisdale John Duff was made prisoner by Colonel Strachan's soldiers and was being taken through the Cabrach, *en route* for Edinburgh. He was well known at the public house where they lodged, and gave a hint to the landlord to give the soldiers of his guard plenty of whisky, while he himself took care of the officer! When they were all thus asleep, John Duff went to the stable and finding one soldier asleep across the door, cut his throat with a penknife, took out a horse and mounted it. But to his horror when he had been riding for a short while he heard a thunder of hoofs behind him and knew that he was pursued. He rode all night and when the dawn broke he turned and saw that he was followed by riderless horses. In the dark he had taken one of the troop horses and the rest had come after their mate. Upon that he proceeded to Buchan where he sold the horses and lived quietly in retirement. He married Isobel Pringle.

I met an American once, married to a Pole, I cannot remember her name but I know she acted the title-rôle in *A Lady of Quality* when it was given in London. She told me that she had known plenty of Duffs, Gordons, and Grants in Louisiana and other Southern states descended from Scotsmen sent out as slaves after the Fifteen and Forty-five.

One Duff ancestor went to Sweden and one of my sisters still has a couple of curious old Swedish chairs that he brought back with him. When I was in Sweden at twenty-one, we saw a Duff who was the Consul at Göteborg and I wondered whether he was any relation, but my eldest brother, who is keen on genealogy, maintained that he was not.

I know very little of my grandfather, James Grant Duff, who must have been an amazingly interesting person, but my father and he did not get on, and my uncle, Ainslie Grant Duff, who inherited his mother's property and changed his surname to Ainslie, was not in the least interested in the past. I have this delightful letter written by James Grant Duff to Huntly Gordon, Scott's secretary, describing Banff society in 1828:

MY DEAR GORDON,—
I feel particularly obliged by the kindness which dictated your letter of the 12th. I would have replied to it on receipt but I waited a few days that I might take advantage of your frank and accordingly I enclose the letters which pray send to the 27 post. We are angry with you for giving us no account of your progress and adventures since the departure of Mr. Lushington— pray what situation have you got?—it will give all your many friends here great pleasure to learn that your prospects are comfortable. Mrs. Ainslie gave me an account of your cousins and I sincerely hope William, now commenced on his own account, may be successful. Pray remember us kindly to them both. I have seen some of the *Modern Traveller* but not the part 'of India',

it is of course gratifying to be quoted by such a person as you describe the Editor—the Mahratta history has little merit but its facts, which were sifted from a great mass of rubbish. On that account it will always be of some use as a book of reference—I often felt that I could have written with far more spirit had the subject been likely to be interesting to the generality of readers.

Banff has of late been very gay—the theatre has been a favourite resort and now we have Miss Noel giving concerts—Lord Fife the great supporter of the performers; and all the good-looking girls of the place are liberally supplied with tickets—I saw your friends the Leslies two days ago—Mrs. Leslie only tolerably well. William Gordon Tillynaught and his sister-in-law are in this quarter and a larger addition to the family party at Forglen consisting of Robert Abercrombie, his family and American cousins—at Craigston also they have inmates, and of course we have all in consequence a great deal of visiting going on—I myself am become a regular clod-hopper and shall perhaps be enlightening the world with an essay on live stock by and bye—I don't know——

'On rearing of Swine' it is not a bit more inviting than the Progress of Mahrattas of which I was as sick as I should be of the Pork.

Joined by Dr. and Mrs. Ainslie in our united good wishes and in hopes you will let me know how they are using you—

Believe me—Yours sincerely,
JAMES GRANT DUFF

Eden, *July* 27*th*, 1828

My grandfather was at Banff Academy with Lord Byron, who was a kinsman of his through the Gordons of Gicht. He told my father that when Byron was first addressed at school as Mr. Byron, on his accession to the title, he burst into tears.

Every one knows that the poet lived at Aberdeen, but it is not so generally known that he lived in a little house in Banff (later used for many years as the Manse) with his mother, somewhere between the years 1791 and 1796. They lived near the old church-yard, quite close to Miss Gordon of Gicht's House, 21 High Shore, often called Shore House, which is now in my possession. The latter was built about 1727 by the then Provost. I do not know how it passed into the hands of the Gordons, but Miss Gordon certainly lived there a long time, and when she died left it to Lord Byron, who only held it for a few months, and then, hearing that two female cousins were in distressed circumstances, made it over to them. It pleases me very much to think how constantly he must have been in my house and garden when he was a child, and it seems rather dreadful that the home in which he actually lived with his mother during those years which must have been so vital to his genius, should be literally crumbling away. The wild coast of Tarlair and the great seas breaking over Banff Harbour were probably much more savage than anything Byron can have seen at Aberdeen, and one imagines that his sojourn at Banff must have given definite bias to that attachment to Scotland which is undisputed. A few hundred pounds would buy the little Manse, and a few hundred more would provide a caretaker. The upkeep of the place would be ensured by making it a museum of Byron relics and charging so much for admission and tea. I wish some public-spirited person would start such a fund.

When my mother married there were two

old aunts who still lived in Banff who were great characters, Jane and Mary. They were sisters of James Grant Duff and could have told any amount about the family if any one had cared to find out.

My maternal great-grandfather, Sir Whitelaw Ainslie, held a big position in Madras and wrote the *Materia Medica of India*. James Grant Duff started for that country in 1816, was wrecked off the Cape of Good Hope and saved by a boat sailing to South America. He landed in Buenos Aires where he saw the Inquisition still sitting. He then went to India, having lost all his family papers and all his valuables in the wreck. He fought through the Mahratta War and wrote the classic on the subject, and then was Resident for some time at Sattara. Having suffered in health, he came home, and married Miss Ainslie, Sir Whitelaw's daughter, who was rather a dull young woman with a very handsome and attractive mother who had been a Miss Cuninghame, whom he took to Eden House, Banff.

I expect it was the habits of the time and not the climate that affected him, for he used to boast that he was the only man in his regiment who ever walked to bed, and he drank a bottle of port every night.

My father's brother Ainslie was the only other son, and a daughter Alise, who was adored by both brothers. Ainslie became a diplomat and married a beautiful Miss Morgan, the daughter of a Petersburg merchant. She is still, at over eighty, a captivating woman. He soon became bored with the diplomatic service, and retired to Delgaty Castle, Aberdeenshire, where he lived to be one of the last of the real old Lairds. I do not wonder that Delgaty contented him—few places are more exquisite and from the days when some one wrote,

> 'There be six great baronies in the North
> Fyvie, Findlater and Philorth,
> And if ye wad ken the other three
> Pitsligo, Drum and Delgatie.'

it has been a place of romance and has held the imagination of its tenants.

His youngest son is the best shot in the North of Scotland and a charming fellow who writes capital light verse. Their sister Rachel had beauty, though not as great as that of the mother. She had a gift for painting which she never developed as she might have done, being the only girl and much wanted at home. The eldest son, Douglas, translated Croce, and has also written verse. In fact it would be difficult to find any member of the family who has not at one time or another written verse. My grandfather James wrote a poem, 'To a young lady, found by accident in a chaffinches' nest', which I always found an enchanting proposition. He was a very serious landowner in the days when most men took such a position lightly. He introduced the shorthorn into the North of Scotland, and the Eden herd was very famous.

I had always been fond of my father, and what Adrian told me that Christmas about our forbears interested me immensely—so that when in the summer of 1886 he came back from India, I was prepared to be thrilled by him.

In July we set off together on a round of visits, to Mrs. Humphry Ward at Fox Howe and Mrs. Russell Barrington at Herds Hill and various other places. The visit to Fox Howe was enchanting. Mrs. Humphry Ward was writing *Robert Elsmere* and read and discussed it with my father, and we went to see all the Wordsworth relics and heard endless talk of him. Mrs. Humphry Ward was a fine woman, dignified, kind and extremely thoughtful, though she never seemed to me a very sensitive person. But years afterwards when I was a middle-aged woman I happened to be sitting with her and we were talking about a mutual friend who had just had a baby and I said, 'I am so sorry for her because I remember, for a year after my first child was born, I was so terribly upset by the horrors I had gone through that I never could bear to see a woman in the street who was going to have a baby; I used to go home and cry.' Mrs. Humphry Ward's eyes filled with tears and she took hold of my hand and said, 'Oh, my dear, did you feel like that, I felt just like that too and I thought it was just morbid and that other people could not understand it.' I was very much touched because with all her warm-heartedness and extraordinary gifts, that sort of sensitiveness was not what one would have expected. It comes out in one of her novels, *Lady Rose's Daughter*, which I always think the best thing she ever wrote.

One wet afternoon the door opened and

one of the most beautiful girls I ever saw came in, shaking the raindrops off her hair. It was Jean Graham, whose face was so well known afterwards from the portraits Shanon painted of her.

Then we went on to Herds Hill and that was wonderful too. Mrs. Russell Barrington showed me Watts and Leighton studies, de Morgan tiles and pots, and drawings by Rossetti and Burne Jones, all the world of the pre-Raphaelites in fact.

She, thank God, is still alive as I write, a perfect example of all that was most vital in Victorianism. She was the great friend of Watts and Leighton and Evelyn de Morgan and a host of other interesting men and women, and she had very considerable gifts herself both as painter and as writer. Had she gone through the mill as a young girl and really studied art I think she might have been a very gifted painter, but she had a great fund of hero worship and she copied the pre-Raphaelites and had their faults, the want of reality and the conventionality which characterize any one who goes to other pictures for their inspiration and not to life itself. But her landscapes are often enchanting and I wish she had stuck to them

ALISE GRANT DUFF, LATER MADAME OBRIST

and never attempted figures. Her home in Melbury Road was the only Morris house I ever saw which gave complete satisfaction. It was like the inside of a shell in colour, and although too full as all Victorian houses were, it was the fullness of abundant life and vitality. Emilie Barrington saw so much, and liked so much in this mad, queer, beautiful world that she had to grab it with both hands and line her nest with it. Music, painting, literature, drama, nothing came amiss, and she handed it on with truly royal generosity to every one she came in contact with. All my life 4 Melbury Road was a delightfully fruitful spot to me and it was with a sad heart I said good-bye to it when my dear old friend removed to Herds Hill for good. I was seventeen and a half, and the first and most important quarter of my three score years and ten was over.

It was exciting being with my father again and I think he was glad too, to realize that in spite of my many faults, I had a keen intellectual interest in most of the things he cared about. He was a difficult man to live with in spite of his great charm and brilliant gifts, and I was probably the only one of his children who ever felt at home

A VICTORIAN CHILDHOOD

with him. He was the last man in the world who ought to have had a large family; children meant nothing to him, though he had a great feeling of responsibility towards them. But they tired and bored him, and not being a rich man they meant continual worry about money. Had he not been so continually handicapped by trying, indeed almost having, to live beyond his means, he would, I think, not only have led a much happier life, but would have been able to do and be many things to which he never attained. He was as brilliant as the best men of his day, but he had three great drawbacks to contend with—weak health, shocking eyesight and small means.

My mother, who had iron health and was also very gifted (she wrote admirable poetry and painted charmingly), was a poor manager and bored with domestic details, though she loved having children. So we spent too much on luxuries and had to go without the things that mattered. I suppose no reform ever started has done as much good as the limitation of families even in the hundred years that it has been practised.

My father's sister Alise had married a Swiss, the last descendant of an old patrician family at Zurich, Dr. Obrist. He took this beautiful Scotch girl, who had always lived in great luxury, to live in the exquisite old Obrist Haus at Zollikorn, near Zurich. But she had never realized that life out of the British Isles is a very different matter from life in these islands and that everybody on the Continent, except a few people of the highest aristocracy and a few of the newly rich, are all expected to work and *do* work. She hated the household drudgery which is shared by mistress and maids in most Continental countries, she was shocked to find that nobody dressed for dinner except on special occasions, and although she was delighted with the artists and other interesting men and women she met, for her husband was a gifted man scientifically and a marvellous musician, she felt out of it all and wretched. After some years she left her husband and retired with her two very brilliant sons, Hermann and Aloys, to Weimar. Two even more interesting children had died and the loss of Leila, the little girl, broke her heart. For Max, the most remarkable of them all, she never cared.

One of the most arresting pre-war novels in Germany was written about my aunt and her two sons and their life at Weimar—*Frau Bürgelin und ihre Söhne*. It was written by Gabriele Reuter, who first made her name by *Aus guter Familie*, a strange book, uncannily true but missing a good deal of my aunt's charm. For her charm must have been something quite exceptional. I have heard such different men as Sir James Stephen, Sir George Henschel and Lord Arthur Russell speak of her, and they all said that her beauty, her exquisite voice and her curious dominating personality had made an ineffaceable impression on them. Anyway, I think she has been the greatest influence in my life one way and another. I always longed to know her, but was never allowed to. At last, when I was twenty-one, father said he would take me to her. We started, but the German Empress, hearing he was in Germany, wired for him, and we went round by Homburg. My aunt became suddenly ill and it was all over before we could reach Weimar. I never saw her till she lay dead, a woman of fifty-eight, still beautiful, shrouded in white and covered with great purple clematis flowers.

My father adored her and wrote to her constantly. Her picture hung in the dining-room wherever we went and I was unaccountably attracted to her all my life. I cannot remember when I first began asking questions about her. Unfortunately my mother and she disliked each other, and she never came to stay. Nor were any of us allowed to go and stay with her. But she preoccupied me and when my father found that I was absorbed by Aunt Alise, he used sometimes to tell me about her, though knowing that my mother dreaded her influence, and being very loyal, he generally tried to turn me off the subject. This holidays I remember I returned to the charge. 'What is she like? Why do we never see her? What were my cousins like?' endless questions which my father generally parried by changing the conversation. But Mrs. Barrington could tell me a lot and did.

My mother felt the English climate terribly after India, and it was settled that the family should go abroad for the winter to Syria, where Lawrence Oliphant had lent them his house on Mount Carmel. I begged to be taken, but my mother refused, saying that it was important that my education should not be interfered with. So they arranged that I should go to Smithills for

Christmas and then to Lord Arthur Russell's house in South Audley Street for the rest of the holidays. Lord Arthur was one of my father's dearest friends. And his wife and her mother and sisters, the de Peyronnets, had been friends before her marriage to Lord Arthur.

That visit was a very memorable one and had a far-reaching effect. I loved the whole family, Lord and Lady Arthur, Harold, Flora, Claude, Diana, Gilbert and Conrad. I think they were the happiest family I ever knew. They had none of them been to school. Lord Arthur was very wise and so was his wife, and both had a charming spontaneity and an aloofness at the same time. They were absolutely natural people and always did and said what they liked, for under their courteous exteriors was an iron certainty of what they thought right and wrong and no amount of fashion of pressure from without made them change their minds. They had a wide influence in London and their house was a centre to many people from very varying circles. I had never been in Town except as a small child and Lord Arthur took me to see something new every day. He introduced me to

Limoges enamel and Chinese jade and the toadstools at the National History Museum, and the Elgin Marbles. He explained the characteristics of the Milan, Florentine and other great Italian schools of painting. He took me constantly to the National Gallery and to the London Library and showed me the most famous pictures, and also to the winter show at Burlington House, in fact those three weeks were packed with pleasures. He also renewed my acquaintance with the Piccadilly goat, who had been one of the interests of my infancy, visits to see him causing immense excitement, and as he lived in Hamilton Place quite close to Lord Arthur's house in South Audley Street, I saw him frequently. It is funny how some Londoners do not remember him and non-Londoners simply do not believe in his existence. It was a stock joke between my husband and myself, he averring that it was one of my mental aberrations. Whenever I mentioned the animal he would touch his forehead significantly and say to whoever might be there, 'Poor dear Tiny, you mustn't take any notice of her. She thinks she used to know a goat who lived in Piccadilly.'

Lady Arthur even took me, in spite of my

tender age, to an evening party at Mrs. Earle's, who afterwards became a very dear friend. I cannot remember whether it was at that party, or a few months later at the Ridgeway, Lord Arthur's country house, that I first saw Violet Maxse, the lovely daughter of Admiral Maxse, the original of Meredith's Nevil Beauchamp, afterwards Lady Edward Cecil and later Lady Milner. She was an enchanting girl, brilliant and amusing. Her elder sister Olive and her father later became great friends of mine and were very good to me. Olive was a most exquisite musician.

It was a couple of years later, staying with Jacques Blumenthal, that I became intimate with Mrs. Earle, Aunt T., and her dear kind husband. She had the same intense motherliness that characterized Nono, but without the slightest religious bias of any sort. Some one once said of her that she brooded over every one with a motherly materialism and it was quite true. She was the most human of creatures, interested in every phase of man and woman kind, in their personal appearance, their mental characteristics, their digestion, and other organs, in everything but their souls. How many boys and girls she has helped and freed from nerves and obsessions, by making them talk simply and naturally about them, what marvellous vitality she had and interest in art and decoration and literature. I loved her very dearly, and her friendship was constant and enduring. And I think of her every day, for in my drawing-room stands an exquisite screen of peacock feathers which she copied from one she saw in Rossetti's studio, and which is a perpetual pleasure to me.

I went back to Cheltenham with a mental indigestion but feeling that I had a new family almost, so kind and helpful had the Russells been. They invited me to stay the next holidays, so my cup of happiness was full. I was allowed to go to the Chamiers for the last Sunday before term. They were old Indian friends and had settled in Cheltenham. Their son George was at home and their daughter Alice whom I had known in India. George fell violently in love with me and though I was not in love with him I was delighted to be made love to again. He proposed to me a year after and though I liked him very much, I refused him, for I did not in the least want to marry. I remember being very distressed at the time, I did not realize how much sooner men get over these affairs than women. I should say 'got', for I am glad to say women take love-affairs more lightly than they did and the misery of 'Peine d'amour' is a thing of the past. Men and women love little and often and the relaxed morals of the day make it all very easy.

The Easter holidays whilst my people were in India were generally spent with a sister of Richard Ainsworth's, Mrs. Graham Browne, at Beulah Hill, Norwood. She was a clever, interesting woman, and both she and her husband Hector were first-rate musicians. That spring they took me to a performance of Liszt's 'St. Elizabeth' at the Crystal Palace. I cannot remember whether Liszt conducted, but I know he was there and came and bowed to the audience in response to the applause. Afterwards I noticed him talking to a short dark man. 'Who is that?' I asked Cousin Hector. 'That is Jacques Blumenthal,' he replied, and I saw for the first time a man who for years was one of my greatest friends.

A week later, on the last day of the holidays, Aunt Fanny, my father's sister-in-law, happened to be lunching with the Graham Brownes and said she would take me to Paddington and put me into the train. On our way we called on two old Miss Macleans, friends of my grandmother's. In the drawing-room was a photograph of Aloys Obrist. I stared—fascinated. Who was it? 'That is your cousin Aloys,' said Miss Maclean. 'I must have it,' I said, 'I must take it back to Cheltenham.' 'You cannot,' said Miss Maclean, '*I* want it.' I insisted and was so obsessed that they let me. Next day came an urgent telegram saying it must be returned at once, my uncle was terrified of what my mother would say, knowing her dislike of Aunt Alise. So I returned it. Later, we were the dearest and closest of friends, but his brother Hermann was even closer. Hermann was not handsome, though curiously attractive to women. But Aloys was as beautiful as a boy could be. Once when he and Hermann were going to Bayreuth, an old musician in the train suddenly said to Hermann: 'Why do you go to Bayreuth, you have Parsifal himself with you?'

My last year at Cheltenham was uneventful and rather a waste of time. I was in the Cambridge class under Miss Sturge. She was a good creature, but we did not get on somehow. She thought me a rotter and I thought her a philistine, so though I was sorry to say good-bye to Miss Beale I was pleased to be leaving. The only thing of any moment that happened was a fight between the authorities and myself on the subject of learning Latin. I refused to learn it if I had to learn with the English pronunciation then in vogue at College. I said (I suppose I had overheard my father say it some time) that the Roman Church was the only body who had gone on with Latin since classical times, and that they were obviously more likely to be correct than anybody else. After much fighting, the matter was referred to Miss Beale and she, though not admitting that I was right, allowed me to learn Italian instead. I am always sorry I did not learn Latin, for no one who does not know at least one classical language is really educated, and the lack of Latin has been a drawback to me all my life. But it would have been useless to learn the curious lingo spoken by Englishmen. Many years after I sent my daughter to a Roman priest to learn Latin and with very little trouble and only two lessons a week, she knew enough in two years to read easily and even talk in Latin. This could be done at all our schools if children in this country instead of being taught the strange jargon which passes for Latin could treat it as a living speech and gain culture.

It was during this year that I read Haweis' *Music and Morals* and *My Musical Life*, and, fired by Miss Eales and Hildegarde Muspratt's glowing accounts of Bayreuth, I became a Wagner maniac. I could imagine no earthly bliss greater than going to the Festspiele, and was terribly disappointed when my mother would not let me go. I did not get there till I was twenty-one. My grandmother had left me a small legacy to be paid on my coming of age and with that I went. It was more perfect than my wildest anticipation.

A pleasant recollection of my last term was the presence in our house of Olga Neruda, the sister of Norman Neruda—Lady Halle, the great violinist. Olga was a very gifted pianist, though not as remarkable a musician as her famous sister, but her playing was a delight, and I used to spend hours in her room. She was very kind about performing to us and we all learnt a great deal from listening to her. The town concerts in those days at Cheltenham were also good. Every one of note came to play and sing there, and before I left I had heard most of the musicians who came to England.

Miss Beale disapproved of the local theatre, probably with reason, for there were never any plays worth seeing at it. But one year Benson and his troup came to the town, and though Miss Beale would not relax her rule and let us go to the theatre, the theatre came to us, and Benson performed Macbeth, Hamlet and, I think, Julius Caesar, in the Great Hall. It speaks volumes for the quality of his company's acting, that even the sight of the three middle-aged gentlemen circling round a waste paperbasket, wearing, as far as I can remember, evening clothes, as the Macbeth witches, did not move us to unseemly mirth.

The acting at College itself was good and I remember especially a dignified and moving performance of the *Alcestis* of Euripides.

I went to see some acting at the Ladies' College on the occasion of Miss Beale's centenary last year. It was very unlike the *Alcestis*. We also constantly acted in our various houses, and had fancy-dress dances which were great fun. Many of the girls drew well and we all had albums in which we pasted photographs of pictures we thought beautiful, interspersed with original drawings by our various friends. Photography was in its infancy and the stationers' shops were full of reproductions of modern pictures by French, German and English artists. There was a gentleman called Faléro we especially admired, and Cabanel's 'Venus' had a great following. Leighton's 'Wedded' was another picture to be found in most albums. 'The Still Silent Past', 'The Present Bitter Sweet', of Herbert Schmaltz, had a large public. There were also some peculiarly bad pictures of the Rhine maidens and of Brünnhilde which we thought exquisite. Our French house Mademoiselle was particularly shocked at what she called 'The British taste for the undraped figure'. She always alluded to my album scornfully as 'Claire's Livre de nudités'. I cannot remember her name, but she was very good to me and so was Fräulein von Kries, a dear, shy little person from Oliva, near Dantzig, who was house German mistress. Both she and her French colleague were much trampled on by some of the girls and they were proportionately grateful to any one who showed them any decent feeling. I remember hearing her say once about Hildegarde Muspratt and me: 'Claire et Hilda ont leurs defauts, mais ce sont des êtres humains.'

There is something tragic about breaking-up prayers at school if you are not going back, and glad as I was to leave, I sobbed bitterly as we sang, 'Oh God our help in ages past'—for the last time, to the tune Miss Beale loved so well. Her successors have returned to the older and doubtless finer tune, but it has not the swing of the one Miss Beale cared about, and there is something tame about the singing of it. How we used to shout the other one!

In July 1888 I left Cheltenham for good.

INDEX

Abercrombie, Lord, 77
Aden, 75
Adrian, see Grant Duff, Lt.-Col. Adrian
Ainslie, Douglas, 174
Ainslie, Sir Whitelaw, author's great-grandfather, 172
Ainsworth, Miss Hannah (Mrs. Edward Webster), author's grandmother, 9, 12, 13, 47, 64, 72
Ainsworth, Mrs. Richard, Nono (née Lily Vaughan), 127, 128, 134, 137, 154, 155, 156, 158, 159
Ainsworth, Richard, 126, 128, 133, 134, 154, 155
Aitken, Miss, 149
Alcock, Sir Walter, 40
Ali, Arab pony, 79, 82
Andersen, Hans, 44
Anne Marie, author's daughter, 165
Antoine, Mère, 90
Arnold, Matthew, 54
—— —— his poem *Calais Sands*, 52, 54
Arthur, see Grant Duff, Arthur
Atkinson, Mr. Breeks, 103
Awdry, Mrs., 108, 121, 122

Bachelor, nurse, 76, 107, 108, 143
Bacon, Mrs. (née Carr), 6
Bagehot, Walter, 57
Bagot, Arthur, 77, 85, 99, 111, 117, 120, 121, 122,
Banff, 141, 165, 169, 172
Barnewitz, Marta, 140
Barrington, Mrs. Russell, 58, 176, 177, 181
Beale, Miss, 129, 130, 133, 145, 149, 161, 188, 190, 192
Bellairs, Miss, 42
Benson, Sir Frank, 190
Beresford, Lord William, 118
Bible, The, 151, 152
Bidie, Dr., 99
Blacas, Duc de, 35

Blumenthal, Jacques, 184, 186
Blunt, Lady Anne, 118
Blunt, Wilfrid Scawen, 118
Bombay, 75, 76
Bond of Sacrifice, The, 37
Boole, Mrs., mathematician, 149, 162
Borns, Dr. Tutor, 59
Borries, Marie von, 146
Broughton, Rhoda, her novels, 107
Brown, 102
Buckinghamshire, Earl of, 2
Buckle, Miss, 149
Buenos Aires, 172
Bunsen, Georges von, 65
Burn, Capt. Charles, 118
Buxton, Mrs. (née Lubbock), 32
Byron, Lord, 170, 171

Carmel, Mount, 181
Carpenter, nurse, 32, 35, 40
Cartwright, Mabel, 149
Cave, Mrs., nurse, 7, 8
Cavendish, Capt. Cecil, 75
Chamier, Alice, 99, 185
Chamier, George, 185
Cheltenham Ladies' College, 129, 130, 133, 145-53, 185, 187-92
Childe, Canon, 161, 162
Childers, Mr., and daughters, 69
Colefax, Lady, 57
Coleridge, Lord, 143
Coleridge, Hon. Stephen, 143
Collier, Mrs. Gerald (née Lily Grant Duff), author's sister, 123, 165
Cometh up as a Flower, 107
Coventry, Blanche, 148
Crane, Walter, his pictures, 56
Craven, Mrs. Augustus, 33, 34, 61
Cromer, Lady, formerly Mrs. Baring, 118
Crown Princess Frederick (later Empress of Germany), 62, 180

Dalhousie, Lord, 77
Daoud Shah, 112

193

d'Aumale, Duc, 54
Dawkins, Boyd, 140
Delgaty Castle, 173
de Navarro, Madame (*née* Mary Anderson), 18
d'Orleans, Duc, 54
de Peyronnets, the Misses, 182
Dilke, Sir Charles, 65
Doda Bet, 115
Don Juan, Byron's, 44
'Dot', see Grant Duff, Victoria
Dreams, 10-12, 48-49
Droog Mountain, 116
Duff, John, of Bowmakellach, 166
Duffs, author's ancestors, 165-66

Eales, Miss, 131, 132, 146
Earle, Mrs., 184
Eden House, 8, 53, 172, 174
Erskine, Miss Caroline, 58, 64
Evelyn, see Grant Duff, Evelyn
Ewing, Mrs., her books, 44, 139

Flower, Dinah, 131
Fox Howe, 174
Framjee Pestonjee, 104
François de Sales, Soeur, 90
Frau Bürgelin und ihre Söhne, 180
French, Louis, 16
French, Mrs., author's governess, 16, 27, 49, 68-69
Fritzl, author's son, 71

Gell, Bishop, 98
Gladstone, Herbert, 66
Gordon, Capt., 75, 82-85, 86, 94, 99, 108
Gordon, Huntley, 168
Gordons of Gicht, 170
Graham, Jean, 176
Graham Browne, Gertrude, cousin of Lady Grant Duff, 186
Graham Browne, Hector, married Gertrude Ainsworth, 186
Grant Duff, Lt.-Col. Adrian, author's brother, 4, 11, 14, 15, 22, 29, 30, 31, 35-38, 45, 59, 68, 74
Grant Duff, Ainslie, author's uncle, 168, 173
Grant Duff, Mrs. Ainslie (*née* Morgan), 173
Grant Duff, Arthur, author's brother, 46, 144
Grant Duff, Lady, wife of Sir Arthur (*née* Kathleen Clayton), 144

Grant Duff, Evelyn, author's brother, 21, 22, 143
Grant Duff, Hampden, author's brother, 9, 79, 90, 100, 110, 112, 114
Grant Duff, Iseult, author's sister, 123, 164
Grant Duff, James, author's grandfather, 167-70, 172
Grant Duff, Mrs. James (*née* Ainslie), 172
Grant Duff, Lady (wife of Sir Mountstuart), author's mother, 3, 4-7, 9, 32, 33, 49, 67, 89, 94, 106, 107, 113, 115, 129, 138, 145, 178, 181
Grant Duff, Sir Mountstuart E., author's father, 14, 52, 54, 71, 76, 79, 87, 88, 115, 122, 141, 165, 177
— — his diary, 52, 53
Grant Duff, Rachel Ainslie, 165, 173
Grant Duff, Victoria ('Dot'), author's sister, 62, 72, 100, 108, 109, 117, 123, 164
Grants, author's ancestors, 166
Green, J. R. and Mrs., 65
Greg, Mrs., 55
Greg, W. R., 57
Greg, Walter, 56
Griffin, Townshend, 72
Griffiths, Maud (Mrs. Alford), 63
Grigg, Mr. and Mrs., 99
Grimms' *Fairy Tales*, 44
Guindy, Madras, 78, 86, 89, 105, 117

Haldane, Lord, 37
Ham House, 61
Hamilton, Sir Ian, 95
Hampden, George Cameron, 6-7
Hampden House, 2-7
Hare, Miss Amy, 159
Harry, groom, 8
Haweis, Anglican Clergyman and musician, 189
Henley, Lady, 63, 64
Henschel, Sir George, 180
Herbert, Colonel Kenney, 81
Herds Hill, 176, 177
Hill, Dr., Bishop of Sodor and Man, 140
Hobart, Lady (*née* Carr), 6-7
Hoering, Herr, author's German tutor, 35
Houghton, Lord, 54

INDEX

Hudson, Sir James, 63
Hughes, Arthur, 4
Hungerford, Mrs., her novels, 107
Hunter, Sir William, 99
Huxley, T. H., and family, 72
Hyderabad, 118, 119

Imitation of Christ, The, 45
India, 71, 75, 76, 87, 90
Installation of the Nizam of Hyderabad, 118, 119
Iseult, *see* Grant Duff, Iseult

Jackson, Anna, cousin of author's mother, 33
Jane Eyre, 58
Jennings, the Rev., 25
Jowett, Dr. Benjamin, 65
Jusserand, M. Jules, later French Ambassador to Washington, 107

Kartary, 116
Keyes, Kitty, 123
Kinglake, A. W., 63
Kipling, gardener at Knebworth, 20, 30, 31
Knebworth, 16, 18, 20, 28, 81
Kneller Hall, 61
Knott, Miss, 145
Konradin, author's daughter, 70
Kramer, Mlle., 145

Labouchere, Mrs., 66
Lacaita, Sir James, 63
Lady of Quality, A, 167
Lady Rose's Daughter, 175
Langtry, Lily, 66
Laurie, Miss, 133
Le Chat parti, les Souris dansent, 92
Lily, *see* Mrs. Gerald Collier
Liszt, The Abbe, father of Cosima Wagner, 186
Longfellow, Henry Wadsworth, 49
Lonsdale, Miss, 99
Lubbock, Sir John, afterwards Lord Avebury, 25, 32
Lyall, Sir Alfred, his *Old Pindari*, 50
Lyon, Peter, 166
Lytton, Lady, 19
Lytton, Lord, 18, 20

Macaulay, Lord, his poems, 50
MacDonald, George, his *Fairy Tales*, 44

Mackenzie, Dr., 75
Mackenzie, Etta and Maud, 75, 84, 110, 111
Mackenzie, Mrs., 111
Maclean, Dr., 87, 96
Madé, governess to Maud Walpole, 140
Madras, 76, 117, 122
Mahratta War, 76, 170, 172
Mallet, Sir Louis, 4, 60
Mallet, Lady, 60, 61
Malortie, Baron and Baroness, 66
Malta, 75
Man, Isle of, 138, 141
Marie de Rieux, 92
Marly Mund, 115
Marseilles, 124
Marsh, Richard, Protestant Martyr, 133
Martin, Colonel, 99
Martin, Gertrude, 99
Martin, Grace, 96, 99
Maunder, nurse to author, 7, 8, 30, 31, 32, 35, 44
Maxse, Admiral, 184
Maxse, Olive, 184
Maxse, Violet, afterwards Lady Milner, 184
May, Sir Erskine and Lady, 69
Mettapoliam, 89
Meymott, Miss, later Mrs. Rylands, 39, 40
Milner, Viscountess, formerly Lady Edward Cecil, 184
Minty, Mrs., 13
Mold, Miss, 145
Montefiore, Leonard, 61
Morte d'Arthur, 42, 43
Moss Bank, 135
Moxon, Miss, 96, 100, 101
Muhurrum Festival, 104
Mun, Albert de, 35
Muspratt, Hildegarde, 148, 160
Mustapha Supérieure, Algiers, 32, 33
Mysore, Maharajah of, 113, 114

Napier of Magdala, Lord, 55
Naseweis und Däumelinchen, 62
Necklace of Princess Fiorimonde, The, 56
Neddiwattum, 116
New Forest, 69, 70
Nilgiris, Hills in Southern India, 94
North Lodge, Ealing Green, 9, 12

Obrist, Aloys, 179, 187
Obrist, Frau Alise, 173, 178, 179, 180, 181
Obrist, Hermann, 187
Obrist Haus, Zollikon, near Zurich, 179
Obrist, Leila, 179
Obrist, Max, 179
Oliphant, Laurence, 181
Omar, Arab pony, 79
Ootacamund, Madras Hill Station, 89–96, 100, 105, 112, 117
Owen, Sir Richard, 65

Paris, Comte de, 54
Paris, 33
Paris, Notre Dame de Sion, 33
Park Lodge, Wimbledon, 55
Patience, 81
Pattison, Mrs. Mark, afterwards Lady Dilke, 65
Pembroke Lodge, Richmond Park, 62
Peprel, butler to author's grandmother, 12, 47
Perceval, The Misses, 13
Peri, Shetland pony, 8
Pigott, Esmé, 159
'Pigs', game, 70
Pixie, Shetland pony, 8
Plato, 161
Pogson, Mr., Astronomer, 99
Port Said, 75
Pride, Miss, 95
Primrose, Sir Henry, 119
Punch, 58

Récit d'une Soeur, Le, 34
Reinking, Fräulein, governess, 27, 28, 32, 73
Reuter, Gabrielle, German novelist, 180
Ripon, Lady, 118
Robert Elsmere, 174
Roberts, Ladies Edwina and Aileen, 95
Roberts, Sir Frederick, afterwards Lord, 95
Robertson, Miss Margaret, 152
Rossignon, Gabrielle, 149
Ruchet, Mlle., 145
Russell, Lord Arthur, 17, 18, 182–83
Russell, Lady Arthur, 182, 183
Russell, Bertrand, 62

Russell, Claud, 182
Russell, Conrad, 182
Russell, Diana, 182
Russell, Flora, 182
Russell, Frank, Earl Russell, 62
Russell, Gilbert, 182
Russell, Harold, 182
Russell, Rollo, 63
Russell, Lady, widow of Lord John, 62
Russell, Lady Agatha, 62
Russell, Lady William, 17

Sandwith, Gladys, 131
Schmidt, Fräulein, 145
Schübnall, Fräulein, 39, 56, 59, 60
Scowcroft, Lily, 148
Seaford, 47
Sebastian, Mère, 92
Servant of All, The, 58
Smith, Henry, 65
Smithills Hall, Bolton-le-Moors, 9, 133–37, 153–59
Snagge, Judge, 68
Soulsby, Miss, 149, 150, 151, 152, 161
Spencer, Colonel, 94
Spot, dog, 8
Standen, Rev., 136, 137, 155, 156
Stephen, Sir James, 142, 143
Sterling, Miss Amy Hutchisson, 152
Story of an African Farm, The, 160
Strachey, Mrs. St. Loe (née Simpson), 72
Stradiot, Monsieur, 87
Strauss, Johann, his waltzes, 72
Suez, 75
Swinburne, his *Poems and Ballads*, 160

Tabley, Lord de, 64
Tagg, James, coachman, 80, 100, 102
Tarrants, the Misses, 99
Tata, Sir Ratan, 54
Taylor, Dr., friend of Dr. Johnson, 13, 14
Thring, Kate, 69
Travels in Tibet, Abbé Huc, 41
Turgenieff, Ivan, 122
Turner, Amy, 148
Tyndall, John, 61

Verdi, his opera, *Aïda*, 126
Villiers, Mrs., 19
Vuillamet, Mlle., 73

INDEX

Walpole, Lady, 63
Walpole, Maud, now Mrs. Holland, 63, 138
Walpole, Sir Spencer, 63
War Book, 37, 38
Ward, Mrs. Humphry, 174, 175
Webster, Edward, author's grandfather, 8, 9
Webster, Mr., 96

Weimar, 180
Westbourne Place, London, 125
Williams, Joséphine Evans, 148
Wilson, James, 57
Winwick Warren, 126
Wood, Mrs. Henry, her novels, 107

York House, Twickenham, 40, 52, 53, 54, 60, 67, 143

Printed in Great Britain by
Butler & Tanner Ltd.
Frome and London